Black Lives Made a Difference

Fanning the Flames of Revival

Other books by Pamela Bolton:

Ushering in Revival and Awakening—Fanning the Flames of Revival

God on the Move—Fanning the Flames of Revival

Circuit Riders—Fanning the Flames of Revival

Lady Preachers—Fanning the Flames of Revival

Today's Glory Stories—Fanning the Flames of Revival

Other books by Dean Braxton:

In Heaven!—Moments in Heaven

A Woman's Stand—Moments in Heaven

What It Feels Like to Die—Moments in Heaven

"I Need You There" Sang the King—Moments in Heaven

Deep Worship in Heaven—Moments in Heaven

En el Cielo!—Serie Momentos En El Cielo

Black Lives Made a Difference

Fanning the Flames of Revival

By
Pamela Bolton
and
Dean Braxton

Copyright © 2025
by Pamela Bolton and Dean Braxton
Black Lives Made a Difference
Fanning the Flames of Revival
by Dean Braxton and Pamela Bolton
Printed in the United States of America

1st Edition
ISBN: 978-1-7349220-1-1

All rights reserved. The author guarantees all contents are original and do not infringe upon the legal rights of any other person or work. No part of this publication may be reproduced or transmitted in any form or by any means, electronic or mechanical, including photocopying, recording, or any information storage or retrieval system, without the permission in writing from the authors.

All scripture quotations are taken from the King James Version
or the New King James Version of the Bible
Copyright © 1982 by Thomas Nelson, Inc., Nashville, Tennessee, United States of America

BLACK LIVES MADE A DIFFERENCE
FANNING THE FLAMES OF REVIVAL
CONTENTS

DEDICATIONS ....
FOREWORD..
INTRODUCTION ....

1. God's Heart for Revival and Awakening 1
2. CLARETTA NORA AVERY Child Evangelist 9
3. John D. Rockefeller's Preacher CHARLES WALKER 25
4. The "Black Billy Sunday" 31
5. Black Women in Ministry 37
6. Young Gentlemen 43
7. Healing Evangelists 49
8. Entire City Shuts Down to Honor Man of God 53
9. Early Giants of Faith in America 55
10. BLIND BUTLER Singing Evangelist 61
11. GEORGE WASHINGTON CARVER 63
12. Destined for Greatness 69
13. HARRIET TUBMAN Woman of Deep Faith and Modern-day Moses 83
14. What Are You Called to Do With Your Life? 89

IN CLOSING...93
BIBLIOGRAPHY 95

DEDICATIONS

Pastor Pamela Bolton

This book is dedicated to all of my family, friends, and ministry contacts who have black skin tone, including but not limited to my nieces, Elizabeth Swain and Lily Foster; my daughter-in-law, Jenise Lemon; friends and mentors, Dean and Marilyn Braxton; Michelle Adams; David Waako; Minister Faye Cohen; Pastors Denise and Darrell Perkins; and Dr. Sonia Lott. I am honored that each of you are a part of my life. You are all amazing!

Jenise is the love of my son Sam Merriman's life, and she is now a part of our family. She is smart, talented, fun-loving, and dependable; and I am thrilled to welcome her to our family as my daughter-in-love.

I also want to thank my mother, Barbara Griffin, for raising me to love everyone and appreciate each person individually, not basing their value or worth on the color of their skin, the community they grew up in, or their level of education.

Also, I want to thank Liz Bates, because she reviewed this book and gave me her honest opinion about its contents. Her words brought great encouragement to me and helped me to move forward in the direction of finally getting this book published.

Evangelist Dean Braxton

I would like to dedicate this book to my mother Freddie Mae Braxton. She made a substantial difference in my life as a child and an adult. At the time of the release of this book she is 91 years old and still active in her church, Mount Olive Missionary Baptist Church in Atwater, CA.

For many years, she also headed up food giveaways out of her church. I remember times of being with her as she would drive to the local food bank, seven miles away, to get food. She then would drive back to her church and organize the food by putting it in bags with others helping her. This was all done on the same day, to be able to give the bags away to people who needed food in the area. She was also the secretary of her church for many years and took care of the administration responsibilities. She also was on the Mother Board and involved in Women's Mission. In her community and church, she became a spiritual mother to many young people. She is still fulfilling that role in many people's lives to this day.

As I stated earlier, she is still active in her church and community in promoting the Kingdom of God.

Thank you, Mom, for being an African American woman who made a difference in my life as well as in the lives of many others.

FOREWORD

Black Lives Made a Difference is a book that I chose to partner with Pamela Bolton on so that we can get this information out about African Americans who are mostly unknown in their contribution that has enhanced the Kingdom of God in the world. My personal reason for doing this book is because of the significance that many African Americans, men and women apostles, prophets, evangelists, pastors, and teachers had on my life.

In this book, you will find some known and some not well-known African American ministers who made a substantial impact on today's direction in promoting the Kingdom of God on earth. I, as an African American evangelist for Jesus Christ, have taken the responsibility that my own family was given to proclaim the Good News, as my ancestors have done for years.

Even in my own family lineage, there are many people who shared the Gospel, the Good News of Jesus Christ. On my mother's side, there was my great-great-grandmother Broussard who was a Pentecostal missionary in Mexico in the early 1900s. There was my grandpa, Deacon Freddie Begron, and my grandmother, Deaconess Mary Deblaw, who also served Christ with great love for Jesus in Pleasant Grove Missionary Baptist Church in Houston, TX, in the mid-1900s. My grandmother, Mary, is the one that I met in heaven who told me to bring back as many of my family members as I could so we could all be together forever as a family. Then there is my own mother, Freddie Mae Braxton, who is active at Mount Olive Missionary Baptist Church in Atwater, CA. She is still serving in her church to this day at 91 years old. Then on my father's side, there is my great-great-great-grandpa, Rev. Lewis B. Braxton, out of Kingston, Tennessee. I'm putting a short article below about him promoting the Kingdom of God through education. His oldest son, my great-great-grandpa, Thomas Braxton, was a minister like his father before him.

Since I know that prayers do not expire or as I like to say it, "have a shelf life," I know I have benefited from many of these men and women of God in my family history, who promoted the Kingdom of God, to the point that the following statement is not only my calling but may have been my family's calling for generations.

The Spirit of the Lord is upon me, because He has anointed me to preach the Gospel, The Good News, to the poor (Luke 4:18)! To tell everyone in the world of His Great Love for them. My goals are to show, tell, and remind people of This! For God so loved (them) the world that He gave His only begotten Son, that whoever believes in Him should not perish but have everlasting life. For God did not send His Son into the world to condemn the world, but that the world through Him might be saved. "He who believes in Him is not condemned; but he who does not believe is condemned already, because he has not believed in the name of the only begotten Son of God." (John 3:16-18). He has sent Me to heal the brokenhearted, To proclaim liberty to captives, and recovery of sight to blind, to set at liberty those who are oppressed; To proclaim the acceptable year of the Lord (Luke 4:18-19)... all in the Authority of Jesus Christ.

The following short article of my great-great-great-grandfather's life shares the love of God that has been poured out in my own family over the generations.

REVEREND LEWIS B. BRAXTON

Education is a family value with deep roots. Lewis Braxton contacted the Freedmen's Bureau, in 1867, seeking a teacher for the freed Black community in Kingston, TN. The following passage, excerpted from a 2009 UT Knoxville

Master's thesis details his efforts: "...Unlike white teachers, black educators could be incorporated into the community at large. At Kingston, Tennessee, where freed people could barely clothe and feed themselves, the local black leader, Lewis Braxton, downplayed their poverty because 'most of us appreciate the importance of educating our children.' With a structure in place and eager to begin classes, Braxton appealed to the Freedmen's Bureau for a teacher. 'Kingston's freed community would be well satisfied with white instructors,' he wrote 'but would be unable to pay for their separate accommodations.' Braxton, instead, outlined a plan where such members of his community who were financially able would 'take the teachers first in one family, and then in another [so that] the burden would fall on a very few of us.' Although Braxton could only guarantee sparse accommodations, his town would expect to do all in our power to make them as comfortable as we could, and as our limited means would allow."

1805 – 1889

The **Reverend Lewis B. Braxton** founded Braxton Chapel in Kingston, TN, on December 24, 1874, six years after his son, Edward Braxton, donated the land for the church. The original church building was replaced with a new one, on the same property, decades later. The new church building has since been remodeled, and the church is still in operation today.

Many family members are buried in the cemetery on the chapel grounds, including Lewis Braxton, Rev. Lewis B. Braxton.

1805-1889   Braxton Chapel (1875) is still in operation today.

Missionary Broussard   Deacon Freddie Begron   Deaconess Mary Deblaw

As you have read, these relatives of mine have made a big difference in my life for the Kingdom of God. They are now part of that great cloud of witnesses that are looking down from heaven cheering me on, as I move forward in promoting God's Kingdom.

If I stop here, I do a dishonor to the other African American men and women apostles, prophets, evangelists, pastors, and teachers who have poured into my life over the years. I'd like to mention their names in honoring them. Elder Andrew Brown, Grace Tabernacle Church, Fairmead, CA; Bishop Dwight and Pastor Gwen Amey, New Faith Tabernacle, Merced, CA; Pastor Naman Lewis, Mount Zion Missionary Baptist Church, Merced, CA; Pastor Williams, Eastside Baptist

Missionary Church, Wichita Falls, TX; Pastor Roger Taylor, Mount Olive Baptist Church, Atwater, CA; and Apostles Tony and Cynthia Brazelton, Victory Christian Ministries International, Woodbridge, VA.

As you have read, Black apostles, prophets, evangelists, pastors, and teachers MADE an enormous difference in my life. That is why I encourage you to read *Black Lives Made a Difference*.

Evangelist and Author Dean A. Braxton

INTRODUCTION

For years, we have had a passion to see our country break out in full-blown revival and awakening. Many others share the same desire, and many people from all over the United States have been praying to see this in our day. God desires that we fan the flames of revival – wherever we are, and we hope that this book will help do this. We are all called to dig up the old wells of revival and pray for fresh living water today.

We are fascinated by the stories that are included herein, because they share details of the lives of courageous, black men, women, and young people who pushed past cultural limitations and made a difference for the Kingdom of God. Some of their lives have had an effect on our lives today. It's time to bring these accounts together in one book so that people can be encouraged to live up to their God-given potential today.

Our prayer is that this book will help bring healing and unity among the people of God as we look forward to what will likely be the greatest revival in all of history.

IT REALLY IS ALL ABOUT JESUS!

PLEASE NOTE: Any time that you see text in italics in Chapters 2-13, it is either Pamela or Dean's writing. All other text in these chapters is directly quoted from old newspaper articles, which are then cited at the end of each section of print. Some minor grammatical and spelling errors were corrected from the original newspapers, for clarity; and any place that you see *Black* or *black* in italics, it is replacing a derogatory term for a Black person.

Chapter 1
God's Heart for Revival and Awakening

God is the God of revival and full-blown awakening! It's aways about Him, His love for people, and His desires being fulfilled on the earth.

He's always looking for that one person who is sold out for Him. It's His heart's desire for all to serve Him with their whole being. Throughout history, God has used anyone who was willing to do whatever He called them to do, despite whether they were born into wealth or poverty, despite the color of their skin or their education level. Today, He's still the same, and His desire is for people to come into relationship with Him and walk out His call for their lives.

WHERE DO I BEGIN?

Let me start by saying that I love studying the history of what God has done in an area, about old revivals and awakenings, and about places where God has moved in power. So, I'm going to begin right here where I am now. In December of 2024, I was voted in as the next pastor (the second woman pastor) of a little country church in upstate New York – the South Granville Congregational Church.

[1]In 1785, Lemuel Haynes became the first ordained black pastor in a Congregational Church within the United States; and for the last 11 years of his life (1822-1833), he

ministered at this little church where I now pastor. It is an honor and a privilege to be able to share the Gospel and serve in the same building where this powerful man of God served.
(Cover photo - Lemuel Haynes - courtesy of the South Granville Congregational Church).

Lemuel was a highly respected minister among his peers, and he was well loved by the congregations that he served for over 50 years.

LEMUEL HAYNES
1753-1833

"God is color blind and all men are equal."
Lemuel Haynes

MY PASSION

Today, my passion is for all people to come into relationship with Jesus Christ and for full-blown revival and awakening to take place in our land. I believe that this is the heart of God for us today, and I also believe that this is the answer to many of the problems that we are facing as a nation, especially the problem of racism; because at its core, it is a spiritual problem. Sometimes people try to fix things in the temporal realm, but you can't fix a spiritual problem with temporal means. I pray that in our day Christians will truly be united as one nation under God, regardless of race or gender, and lead our nation forward in unity. I also pray that forgiveness will be extended wherever bitterness still resides in men's hearts so that all will be free to be all that God desires for them to be.

I have studied and done research about old revivals, and I've written four other books on this topic, because I believe that the old accounts of what God has done in past generations are also our stories… all of our stories. They are our common spiritual heritage. We can be encouraged by them, and if we allow them to, they can help build our faith to believe God for even greater things today.

In each of my books, I relate accounts from old newspaper articles about men and women who were used powerfully by God to bring people into relationship with Him. Many of their stories have long since been forgotten and buried in old newspapers. Each book focuses on a specific group of people who God used to help accomplish His will at a certain time period in history.

MY MOTHER AND GRANDMOTHER

My mom, Barbara Griffin, was brought up in the very well-to-do area of West Orange, New Jersey; and sadly, her mother was extremely prejudiced against people of all races who had any shade of dark skin.

For example, in 1960, my mother made the tryouts for the United States Olympic Team for Track and Field. In the past, she had competed outstandingly well at Madison Square Garden and other large venues, but there was one big problem. The coach was black! My grandmother told my mother that if she went to the tryouts, she would disown her, because it would be a disgrace to the family to have her daughter go with a black coach.

Because of incidences like this one, my mom detested any form of prejudice; and she vowed to raise her children to love and respect all people.

THE HOUSE WHERE I GREW UP

When I was a child, my family lived in an old farmhouse in Cambridge, New York; and we were told that this house had been part of the Underground Railroad. I remember feeling honored and in awe of the fact that likely slaves who were escaping to freedom had stayed in the very building that we lived in.

In the basement, there was a tiny cement room, approximately 5' x 4' x 4', off of a root-cellar-like area that had a very old doll and some old, shredded clothing in it. I remember looking in there and wondering about the people, especially children, who lived in our house and who may have spent time in that little place.

Back then, I was fascinated with the story of Harriet Tubman's life and especially the part about her bravery with helping people escape slavery via the Underground Railroad.

As I began preparing to write this book, I was reminded again about Harriet and what a remarkable, strong woman she was. With this came the memories of growing up in our old house.

So, in November of 2020, I contacted an old neighbor, Marlene Lee, who still lives next door to my childhood home; and she told me that at one time there was a tunnel leading from near the house to the woods on the backside of the property, right along the railroad tracks. When I asked her how she knew about the tunnel, she said that someone in town had told her family about it many years prior. She had moved there as a child in the early 1950s. Although I haven't been able to document the authenticity of this, it backs up what we were told as children.

WHY BLACK LIVES?

God has always used people who have had willing hearts, irrespective of where they were born, who their parents were, their gender, or the color of their skin.

One of my books was about little-known lady preachers and evangelists within the United States who ministered between approximately 1800 and 1925. They didn't have an easy or "fair" life... far from it. Many people came against them, but they persevered; and God used them mightily to make a difference for eternity. Their stories are important, because they encourage women today to find their place and fulfill the call of God on their lives in a world where there is still sometimes prejudice against and poor teaching about women in ministry.

In my third book, *Circuit Riders—Fanning the Flames of Revival*, I shared about men (and a few women) who traveled, often alone, on horseback to bring the Gospel all across this nation between the late 1700s and early 1800s. Many of them faced huge hardships as they rode through the woods on horseback. They faced hunger and danger from wild animals as well as harsh weather conditions. Their passion to share the Gospel surpassed their temporary afflictions. Due to their difficult lives, many of them didn't live to reach the age of 40. I felt that some of their stories, which had long since been forgotten, needed to be brought back into the light to encourage this generation of believers.

In this book, I want to highlight some African Americans who also made a big difference in the history of our country. Many of them overcame insurmountable odds to make a difference for the Kingdom of God. You may not be familiar with some of their names, but I can assure you that they are well known in Heaven, and that's where being known really counts—for all of eternity.

I believe that God created all people, and each one is beautiful in His eyes. In Genesis 1:26-27, the Bible says that all mankind was created in His image. Sometimes on this planet, men judge things based on preconceived ideas and the outward appearance of a person, but God doesn't see things the way that men do. What He's concerned with is what a person's heart looks like.

I pray that you will be blessed as you read the stories of the lives of these Christian men and women of Black heritage who have made a big difference in many areas of society. Some of them were powerful, had great influence, and helped lay the spiritual foundation for this great country, which we are blessed to be a part of today. Many of them faced extremely difficult situations, but with God's help, they overcame.

In a time where we are hearing so much negativity, I hope that this book will be an encouragement to all races concerning the rich spiritual and cultural heritage that Black men and women have contributed to our nation. As you will see, in spite of the prejudices and racial injustices of that time, God still moved to change the hearts and lives of many people.

I have tried to keep all the articles included herein as authentic as possible. They are written word for word as they appeared in old newspapers, because they reflect the reality of the culture of that time in our history. As you will see, it can be very painful to read some of the words used back then to describe people of color. For example, negro, nigger, colored, darkey, pickaninny, and others, so in almost every place that one of these words was used, I have replaced it with Black. I in NO WAY condone the use of this type of language, and I am not in any way in agreement with slavery, the violence, or the derogatory terms that were used back in that day, but I want to present the truth of what happened as accurate, historically, as possible.

I pray that you will be able to look past the terrible language and violence and focus on the great contributions that the men and women who are listed in this book made to our nation. Many of them made a difference that helped to shape the spiritual heritage that belongs to all of us who live here today.

As you read the following accounts, you'll see that as a society, we have come a long way from where we were in the 1800s and early 1900s; and today, we need to take an honest look at where we are now so that we can move forward and do even better tomorrow.

God has special plans for each and every person whom He created, and that includes YOU, dear reader. His plans for your life are not based on the color of your skin but on your willingness to be used by Him. He sees who you are on the inside, and He will use you if you have a willing, pure heart… FOR SUCH A TIME AS THIS.

For years, many people all around the world have been praying and seeking God for full-blown revival and awakening. As we've seen in the past, when this happens, racial division ceases, and people treat one another as true family … the family of God.

"A willing heart opens the door to unlimited opportunities when you put your trust in the One True, Living God!"
PAMELA BOLTON

8

Chapter 2
Claretta Nora Avery
Child Evangelist

Claretta Avery, child evangelist, impacted literally thousands of people. Among them was a squire whose story was recorded in a newspaper in 1895. I am going to begin with this man's testimony, because it is very powerful. Amazingly, Claretta's ministry began when she was just five years old.
                              PAMELA

THE COLORED GIRL PREACHER.

San Antonio daily light. [volume], January 16, 1896, Image 3

A *BLACK* PREACHER
Wonderful Doings of a Little *Black* Girl Evangelist

A South Carolina Squire's Story of the Child Who Is Preaching the Gospel with Such Power to Black and White

A *BLACK* PREACHER

About a dozen prominent members of the Southern colony in New York met in the lobby of a down-town hotel the other evening to talk over old times with a genuine old South Carolina "squire," who is spending a few days in the city, says the *New York Sun*. This gentleman of the old school acquired the title of squire in the old days, when it was a little above that of "judge," and far above that of "colonel," as a mark of popularity and dignity, and he wears it gracefully still.

"Squire, suppose we all take something," suggested the big colonel from Kentucky.

"I can't do it, boys," responded the squire, and a faraway look came into his kindly eyes. "You see, I've stopped."

"Wh-e-w," whistled the colonel, with a long-drawn-out sound like a fall wind. "I can hardly believe you." And every man in the party looked as if he was thinking the same thing, but none made any comment.

"How did such a misfortune come upon you?" finally ventured a Virginian, after the first great wave of surprise had subsided, for they all knew that for nearly forty years the squire had taken his toddy three times daily after meals to aid his digestion.

"Well, boys, it was this way," he said. "The little *black* girl preacher converted me, and I've dropped a good many of my old ways, such as cussin', swearin', and drinkin'. I reckon you maybe all read that little editorial about her in the Sunday's *Sun* suggesting that she should come to New York and preach in Madison Square Garden. Well, all I've got to say is, if she comes, you must all go to hear her; and if her sermon don't touch your hearts more than all the Parkhurstian bombs and Talmagie Roman candles that you've listened to since you moved to this district, then I'll go back to my wicked ways."

"Who'd ever have thought that what a durned little *black* had to say would influence a man of your common sense, squire?" spoke up the oldest man in the crowd, testily. "I wouldn't have believed it of you. What manner of child is she, anyway, and where did she come from?"

"I don't know a great deal about her past history, which is a very short one, as she is only nine years old," commenced the squire, as he took a long draw at a corn-cob pipe, "but she was born near Washington, somewhere in Virginia, I think, in the fall of '85. Her daddy was a preacher and died three or four years ago. This child, whose full name is **Claretta Nora Avery**, has always eagerly attended religious services and taken a great interest in the spiritual welfare of her people. She says that the love of God entered her heart when she was a year and a half old and has never left it, but of course you all won't believe that, for no genuine darky has any idea of time. I'd been hearing and reading a good deal about her and not believing much, and when business carried me to a small town in the lower part of the state, where she was holding a meeting, I decided to go around to the church to hear her. It was quite late, and I got there just in time to catch the last sentence of her sermon.

"I'm going to stay in the field here until I die, and when death comes, sometime, 'way over yonder, where my Jesus is, I'll live there too, singing always that new song with Him in glory.'

"Her voice had a mournful hug in it, and the little creature made a most pathetic picture as her head bobbed up from behind the pulpit and her great eyes roved over the congregation in an appealing way. She looked about her wearily and sadly for a moment, but soon a radiant light fell upon her face, for her sermon had struck home, and she knew it; the entire congregation began to sing, and the queer part of it all was, they began to sing the same thing. Soon some began to chant, while others cried aloud, moaning and bewailing their sins. You talk about your paid choirs. There isn't enough money in New York to buy such music as I heard that night. The voices were rich and full and sweet, and a minor chord that touched one's very soul was the predominating sound.

"Sermons and music have a most electrifying effect upon a *black* congregation, and this one was soon wrought up to the highest pitch of religious excitement. Some of the mo'ners prostrated themselves on their faces, beating the bare floor with their hands until they were worn out, when they would lie in what is termed a trance. Others crawled on their knees to the pulpit. Many of them sat in the midst of this uproar and appeared neither to see nor hear, so intent were they in working out their own Salvation. In the meantime, the old sisters who were sure of Heaven, kept on singing to keep things going. The leader that night was a regular old-time, befor'-the-war mammy, and goodness fairly beamed from her countenance.

"'I bin a li-ar so long, so long—
So long, so long;
I bin a li-ar so long,'

she chanted in a weird, pathetic voice, and every person in the congregation who was able to lift his or her voice chanted the refrain at the end of every three lines:

"'Gin me a little tine ter pray.'

"Everyone was in motion. Some swayed their bodies backward and forward, some shuffled their feet in time to the music, and the very happy ones clapped their hands and shouted: 'Glory, my Lawd!' This kept up for hours. Several prostrate forms were carried out, and a number were left in the church, where they lay until next day. When I got tired and went away that night the little preacher, utterly worn out, had curled herself up in a splint-bottom chair, and was enjoying the sleep of innocent childhood. I could hardly sleep that night for thinking about that meeting. I tell you, boys, 'I was impressed.'

"I always thought you were above such superstition, squire," remarked someone, as the squire stopped to refill his pipe.

"Well, anyway, I went back the next night," resumed the squire, "and for the first time got a good view of the little preacher. She is a perfect child in looks and ways. Her complexion is. about the color of on old mustard ground ginger cake, her teeth white and even, the whites of her large, mournful eyes prominent, and she doesn't weigh more than sixty or seventy pounds. There were a lot of white people in the congregation, but she took no notice of them. Curiosity prompted me to go to listen to her, but interest held me there. She spoke right out in the most earnest way, as if her only thought was preaching the Gospel. Her delivery and gesture were easy, and, in fact, what she said and the way she said it beat nine tenths of the preachers—especially these evangelists—white or black.

"She opened service with a very good prayer, and read, or rather recited, a chapter from the Bible, which did not bear on the sermon in the least, her one thought seems to be to prepare for the Great Beyond, which she designates as 'way over yonder.' She talks about the hereafter in a most pathetic way, and I remember on that particular night her text was: 'Business in Heaven.'

"'I'll meet you there, sinner,' she said, 'for I got business with Capt. Jesus. I must tend to it. I must go where partin' is no mo'. I got to put on a long white robe, a starry crown, silver slippers, and sit at my Master's feet. I'll meet you over yonder, way over yonder, for we all got to cross Jordan stream dry shod and go over yonder. I'll meet you there, sad-hearted mothers. I'll meet you there, wicked fathers. I'm going to get inside those pearly gates. Are you? Are you? Sinner, you must get right. Learn it now. Now is the time. Way over yonder may be too late for you, and so on. Night after night I went, and each time she had a new sermon, each one containing a sad strain.

"She made a pathetic figure, always clad in deepest black without the lightest touch of color, that children love so well, or the faintest suggestion of an ornament. When occasion demanded, she rebuked thoughtless persons for bad behavior in a few clear cut, kind sentences and went right on with her sermon. If the Gospel grinders would only learn that it isn't these staggering truths, which cannot be grasped by the average mind, but a doctrine of simple, earnest faith that arouses people to better living. But they never will, Now it was the sincerity of the little *black*, and the earnestness of her followers, that impressed me, and, while I can't say that she converted me, she certainly set me to thinking, and I concluded to leave off doing certain things.

"I wanted to give her something, and couldn't make up my mind what to buy her. She reads poorly and can scarcely write at all, but somehow, she didn't seem like a child that would care for toys. Finally, in a sort of desperation, I settled on a large wax doll with highly colored cheeks and a mass of yellow hair. If you could have seen her antics of delight when she found that it was all her own. She grasped it to her as if she would never let it go, and then she told me that she used always to preach sermons to her dolls, and that the people who overheard her persuaded her to preach to people, which was the very thing she had always longed to do.

"Everybody agrees that she is a wonder, and I tell you she is. Many white people think her inspired, and the blacks believe that she is sent directly from God as a warning and that the judgment day is coming soon. I don't know, because I've never thought a great deal about such things. But I do think she is entirely different from any little child that I've ever seen, and I shall never, never forget her, with her solemn ways and her unceasing warnings about what we must do and must not do 'if we want to meet each other when we get home, way over yonder.'"

There was a great shuffling of feet, coughing, and clearing of throats among the squire's visitors as he concluded, and the blustering gentleman from Kentucky began to denounce the excise law in loud tones. But the squire looked at the rings of smoke as he blew them upward from his corn-cob pipe and had little to say the rest of the evening.

Herald and News., December 05, 1895, EXTRA SOUVENIR EDITION, Image 6

BLACK GIRL PREACHER
She May Remain Here a Week—
Monday Night's Services

Lenora Avery, the *black* girl preacher, was greeted with another large audience at the A. M. E church Monday night. The house was filled, many standing. Several white people attended the service.

Pastor Walker announced before the service opened that the little girl hoped to stay until Wednesday or Thursday of next week, but it was known yet whether she could remain over Sunday, if she does, she will conduct three services in the courthouse on Sunday, one of which will be for white people. He also stated that he had been trying to get a larger building for her to preach in this week but had not succeeded.

A *Sentinel* man heard the wonderful little girl Monday night. When she arose to announce and line the first hymn, every eye in the house was turned towards her.

After the singing, she offered an earnest prayer on behalf of the service. She then read several verses from the 12th chapter of Isaiah.

Lenora's mother, who is a widow and no less than 60 years old, arose and stated that she wished to introduce her 12-year-old daughter. *She* said she was uneducated, that she stopped traveling twice to send her to school, but that she was taken sick both times. The mother then decided that God would make known to her the proper time to educate the girl. The mother added that her daughter was converted when 18 months old.

Lenora selected her text from the 18th Psalm and 2nd verse: "The Lord is my rock and my fortress, and my deliverer;

my God, my strength, in whom I will trust; my buckler, and the horn of my salvation, and my high tower."

After selecting her text, she closed her Bible and spoke without even notes.

She is a fluent speaker, and though uneducated, she uses good language and many practical illustrations." She said everyone is trusting in someone, either Satan, Self, or God. Those who profess to be Christians should let it be known. She spoke of the work being done by young people and urged parents to teach their children about Christ. She told the parents that if their children did not know what the mourner's bench or religion is, they ought to be ashamed to tell it, as they are supposed to be instructors. She wanted to know what kind of religion parents had, who are trying to get to Heaven themselves and letting their children grow up without knowing anything about God. She also spoke in favor of children becoming members of the church at an early age, saying they were like the young trees—need protection. She said that she believed before the end of time children would take the world for God.

Lenora told about the first revival meeting she ever held. It was at her home in Oxford. She and another little girl were playing church with their dolls when Lenora suggested that they have a prayer meeting every night. The neighbors' children were invited, but most of the parents objected, saying it was nothing but mockery. The meeting was held, however, and in a few nights not only the children but many of the parents were present. **The meeting continued; and it was moved to the church; and before the close, 150 people had made profession.** Lenora closed her discourse by urging all of her hearers to cling to the solid rock, Christ Jesus. She then asked all to sing with her that familiar hymn, "Rock of Ages, Cleft for Me." After prayer by Rev. W. W. Pope, Lenora's mother sang a selection entitled "Hold up Your Light." A collection was then taken.

Lenora told the reporter that their home now was in Carthage, NC. She said that when they left Winston, they would either go to High Point or return home. The little girl is bright and intelligent, and it is a treat to hear her talk as well as preach.
The Western Sentinel., October 21, 1897, Image 2

A *black* girl preacher, nine years old, is creating a sensation amongst the *black* people of Wadesboro. The girl is preaching nightly in the *black* Methodist church. She claims to have been converted when eighteen months old.
The News & Observer., May 29, 1895, Page 3, Image 3

A *Black* Girl Preacher, Nine Years Old, Excites Interest

Charleston, SC, Aug. 9. A. special from Darlington, SC, says: **Claretta Norah Avery**, the nine-year-old *black* girl preacher is creating a sensation here. **She is preaching in the *Black* Baptist Church to tremendous congregations, many of whom are white persons.** Her sermons are remarkable in many respects. She does not appear to be a day over nine years old, weighs not over seventy-five pounds, self-collected and calm in manner, forcible in speech and gesture; talks with simple and natural pathos and speaks with strongest convictions. Her sermons just now are the talk of the town, and she seems beyond question to be a prodigy.
The Evening Times., August 09, 1895, Page 4, Image 4

Claretta Nora Avery, the eleven-year-old girl preacher and evangelist, held our citizens, both white and *black*, spellbound during the past week. She is wonderful in her sermons. She far exceeds the expectations of her audience at every service. Let the criticisms be as they may, in our opinion, she is a God-sent preacher. She touched the hearts of the worst sinners and warmed the hearts of all Christians. She is strict, but sways her audience in love at all times. She is profound in the Scripture, and when delivering her sermons, one would imagine that the very words must be printed upon her heart. She is never found wanting but reaches into her subject far beyond expectations. She did a great work here, and we regret to see her leave so soon after such an interest was manifested at her meeting. **We estimate that from fifteen hundred to two thousand people attended nightly at her meetings.**

The Gazette., August 07, 1897, Image 2

RALEIGH, NC, SEPTEMBER 18, 1897

Snapshots and New Era Institution Sparks

Tarboro and this vicinity has been benefitted, delighted, instructed, and puzzled for the last week or more through the preaching of the "Gospel of Christ" by Claretta Nora Avery, 11 years of age, at the A. M. E. Zion Church. I doubt whether in all this country we can find one pulpit orator that can surpass her, when age and size are taken in consideration. She is truly the wonder of the 19th Century. It stands out prominently that she is Divinely endowed.

The Gazette., September 18, 1897, Image 2

A Wonderful Girl

There were fully 2,500 people at the First Calvary Baptist church, *black***, last night to hear Claretta N. Avery, a young** *black* **girl, apparently about 13 years of age, preach.** She has, during her short career, created a decided sensation throughout the North and South, in many of the cities in which she has preached to thousands of persons, both white and *black*.

Her mother, a woman apparently about 55 years of age, travels with her, and last night, sat beside her on the rostrum and seemed to take interest in all that she said to her auditors.

Before the young girl commenced her discourse, a collection was taken up and hundreds liberally contributed.

After the singing of several hymns, the pastor, Rev. J. C. Daniels, announced that the "wonderful little instrument in the hands of God" would again preach at Calvary this afternoon at 3 o'clock in order to allow the hundreds who had been denied admittance to receive the benefit of her powers. This service will be especially for the whites.

Little Claretta is from Carthage, North Carolina, but her pronunciation is distinctly different from that of the Southern *black*, being doubtless due to her long journey through the Northern States. She spoke in a low voice, though clear to those near her, and the immense congregation was aroused to a high state of enthusiasm when she so intended them to be. She seemed to hold them as in a trance, and they appeared deeply touched and strongly impressed by her prayers to God and her interpretation of His Word.

It was with the greatest difficulty that the Rev. Daniel and his assistants could restore quiet when those in the audience became so enthusiastic over the young girl's teachings as to give vent to exclamations of approval and delight; and she was, in fact, repeatedly interrupted during her discourse; and the pastor found it necessary to appeal for quiet.

In her preaching, she said that the Lord sent many into fields to work for Him and that Satan attempted, often with success, to persuade them to work against Him. There were hundreds of unbelievers who had fallen by the wayside by the persuasion of the devil. The sinners needed to come to Jesus in order to appreciate their real condition. It was dreadful to be a sinner and unconverted to the cause of Jesus Christ; for death comes at any moment and perhaps at a time when it is too late to prepare for an entrance into the pearly gates. This cause should be championed until He forbids us to proceed further.

She pictured hell as vividly presented in the mind of a dreaming sinner, as a place where writhing, hissing serpents found their habitation within the living breast: where the soft spots refused to rest the weary limbs of a traveler, for "in hell there is no rest." The sinner then called upon God for aid. When the dreamer awoke, the visions of damnation still fresh in his mind, he deserted the banner of Satan and fought under the colors of Jesus.

She appealed to her now thoroughly aroused and enthused auditors, to do as the dreamer had done when he "washed in the blood of the Lamb." Old women in the congregation called to the young girl in tones of approval, standing up and gesticulating wildly and even applauding at times. The entire assemblage gave vent to their feelings by murmurings of delight as she described the ascent to the heavenly gates and the entrance to the Kingdom of Jesus Christ. Men and women lost control of themselves in mad enthusiasm at the girl's words when she begged them to fight for God and prepare themselves for the fields of happiness above the clouds. Some pressed toward the front of the church and endeavored to get nearer to the girl, throwing up their hands before her and lingering between a smile and a tear of joyful belief.

At the close of her sermon, she asked those who desired to profess their conversion to the cause to stand; and fully 100 arose. Claretta is undoubtedly a wonderful girl, and to hear her is the only way in which her powers of speech can be properly appreciated.—*Columbia State. March 5.*

The Anderson Intelligencer., March 18, 1896, Image 4

The Girl Evangelist

The young *black* girl evangelist, **Claretta Nora Avery**, who has been creating such a stir among the *blacks* in this state, spent last week in Bennettsville, preaching in the *Black* Baptist Church. During her stay in Bennettsville, your correspondent heard her twice, the first time **she preached by special invitation in the Courthouse to a large audience composed of whites and *blacks* and variously estimated at from 500 to 1,000**. Her text on the former occasion was, "Behold how good and how pleasant a thing it is for brethren to dwell together in unity;" on the latter, "Ye must be born again." She is a most remarkable *Black*. She is only nine years old; yet her pronunciation is distinct; her English is good; her reading is excellent and her delivery easy, graceful, and childlike. There is in her discourses, however, no logical sequence of thought. She is evidently a phenomenon of the "Blind Tom" order. She possesses a remarkable memory, and in her duty has heard hours of good sermons and is able to repeat about one third of each of them. Your correspondent was impressed with the marked similarity between each of the sermons he heard. It is curious, however, to note the superstitions among the *blacks* regarding her, some of them believing that she is an angel sent from Heaven.

The Union Times., September 06, 1895, Image 2

LOUISVILLE

Clara Nora Avery (col.) the little girl preacher of 10 years of age, stopped over at Louisville, and preached for the people 2 or 3 days. A very large number thronged to hear her, and all seemed wonderfully astonished at the oratorical powers

of the child. "God moves in a mysterious way, His wonders to perform."
    The Maryville Times., September 24, 1896, Image 1

Chapter 3
John D. Rockefeller's Preacher Charles Walker

Charles Walker influenced many people in his time on earth. John D Rockefeller, the richest man in the early 1900s, was one of them. As you read the following, you will see that Rockefeller even had many millionaires of his time, come to hear this outstanding preacher.

DEAN

"For where your treasure is, there your heart will be also."
Matthew 6:21

SERMONS OF EX-SLAVE ATTRACT RICHEST MAN IN THE WORLD

Charles Walker, The Man Whose Sermons Please John D. Rockefeller and the $100,000 Church His Congregation Is Building

Augusta, GA, April 11. Golf is no longer the only magnet that draws John D. Rockefeller to Augusta. The Gospel, as well as golf, commands the attention of the "Oil King." Rockefeller, like many other millionaires, comes to Augusta in *the* spring to play golf, but lately Rockefeller has been remaining to hear the sermons of *Charles* Walker, ex-slave and typical Georgia *Black* preacher. Walker is not the kind of polished, oratorical Doctor of Divinity Rockefeller is used to hearing in New York, but the richest man in the world, who has heard the greatest evangelists and theologians in the world says: **"Walker seems to me to have more of the spirit of religion than any man I've ever heard preach."**

Walker, in his Gospel, says nothing about theology, and he never attempts to "confute the creeds." He swings some sledge-hammer blows, though, at sin and the Prince of Sin, and he talks a great deal about the mercy of God.

Walker never changes his sermons or songs to please his wealthy patron. **No matter how many weeks he remains in Augusta, Rockefeller attends Walker's church every Sunday. Other millionaires also attend the Gospel meetings.** The Day Book., April 11, 1916, LAST ED., Images 25 & 26

A FAMOUS *BLACK* PREACHER

Dr. Charles T. Walker,
Pastor of the Institutional Church, Augusta, GA,
Called the Best Preacher in America

PREACHES TO JOHN D. ROCKEFELLER

Aged *Black*, Former Slave,
Has a Firm Friend in the Oil King

John D. Rockefeller finds he can hear the Gospel preached better in Augusta, GA, than anywhere else in the world. And the preacher is a *black*, born a slave. **The richest man in the world sits in one of the front pews reserved for white people, and the congregation sings old hymns as only *blacks* can sing them.** The voices of the women rise in a fine treble, and the bass of the men, repeating the chorus, breaks in with a deep rumble of sound. They sway their bodies slightly, and their voices rise in a chant of praise.

"Swing Low, Sweet Chariot," is followed by "I Shall Be Whiter Than Snow," and then by hymns of their own, which you can hear nowhere but in a *black* church:

"Good Lawd, I wonder,
"Good Lawd, I wonder,
"Good Lawd, I wonder.

"Is anybody here gettin' ready to die?"

"Amen!" says an old man, whose wooly hair is turning gray and who hobbles with a cane.

"Praise God!" exclaims a woman's high voice, and her face lights up with the glory of religion.

The organ drops from the rich, worshipful music to an epilogue of the organist's invention, and the congregation sits back to hear the Gospel preached with a fire that reaches the sinner's heart. And Mr. Rockefeller sits with them.

The preacher, Charles Walker, who has been half-hidden behind the tall stand on which is the big Bible, gets up and looks around at his congregation. He is a very black, plain looking *black*, just like any other Georgia *black*; and he speaks with the richness and the feeling that is inherit in his race.

John D. Rockefeller's example has set a fashion among the rich tourists wintering in Augusta. At times, the *black* preacher, an ex-slave, has a dozen millionaires among his hearers. But he doesn't seem to know they are there. He preaches just the same, delivers the same message of the goodness of God.

Now that Booker T. Washington is dead, Walker is the most remarkable *Black* in the South. He was born in 1858 as the property of Dr. W. A. Clark, who lived in Augusta. The war came on, and the emancipation of slaves followed. He was just a *black* then, and he doesn't remember anything about those times. But he recalls vividly his struggles for an education; and how, at last, he found a place at the Atlanta Baptist College.

He was trained there for a preacher and began even as a young man to be known for his eloquence.

Twice he went to Europe, both times to attend the World's Baptist Alliance; and in London met Dr. Spurgeon, who called him the "preacher from the soil."

In New York, he came to know John D. Rockefeller, who contributed to the educational and religious work the preacher was supporting. This church will be completed in

the fall of this year, will cost about $100,000, and will seat a congregation of 3,000 people.

Mr. Rockefeller, ex-President Taft, and a great many others have contributed to the fund with which the church is being built.

It was Walker's plan to teach sewing at the church, to have a broom factory and a carpenter's shop there, and in every other possible way to make it a help to his people.

He has an advisory board of white citizens of Augusta who aid him with the affairs of the church and who believe he is the wisest leader the *Black* race has today.

Mr. Rockefeller is intensely interested in the church and often writes the pastor about its affairs. The richest man in the world has several times said of the Georgia black who is an ex-slave:

"He seems to me to have more of the spirit of religion than any man I've ever heard preach."—*Philadelphia Record.*

The Kansas City Sun., April 22, 1916, Image 1

CHAPTER 4

THE "BLACK BILLY SUNDAY"

In my research, I found that there were many black men and women evangelists who were referred to as the "black" so and so. For example, some were compared to D. L. Moody, some to Charles Spurgeon, and some to Billy Sunday. I debated as to whether or not to include this in this book because of the current political climate within the United States; however, I decided to cover it, because it is part of our history. The important piece here is not by what name these Godly men and women were known, but that they were used powerfully to impact thousands of people for eternity and that their names are well known in Heaven. PAMELA

EVANGELIST COMING—
WILL STIR DENVER

The Seattle Republican., July 31, 1903, Image 9

REV. J. GORDON McPHERSON, "THE BLACK BILLY SUNDAY," HOLDS ROUSING REVIVAL MEETINGS AT EVANSTON, IL

Black Billy Sunday, the man with a burning message that has thrilled thousands from coast to coast, .has invaded the exclusive strongholds of the multi-millionaires and the near multi-millionaires with his old-time Gospel, and hundreds are crowding the Mt Zion Baptist Church nightly, of which the eminent Dr. E. P. Jones, who is president of the Great National Baptist Convention (unincorporated), is the genial pastor. No evangelist has ever visited Evanston and so stirred the community with such religious fervor as this gifted man of God, while the "Search Light" has attempted to stir up a tempest in a teapot under the bold caption "Jim Crow Revival in Evanston." If there is such a revival in progress in Evanston, the editor of this yellow journal is urged to come to Evanston and locate the same or forever be branded as the man who beat the Devil at his own game and he is the-father of lies. **If reports are true, Black Billy has left meetings down in the *black*-hating South, where the race lines are drawn so close until one could hardly slip a sheet of paper between the lines; and reports from Southern journals have told the story under glowing headlines of the great meetings, where color lines were thrown to the four winds, so anxious have been the people to hear the old Gospel.**

It can be said of Black Billy's work here in Evanston that it has no earmarks of the so-called *black* revivals with old-time grotiousness and whooping 'em up like an Indian war dance with its blood and thunder. **Black Billy is the evangelist of the new order and preaches the Gospel with a punch that makes blacklegs and hypocrites in the amen corners whine, as he sends home his Gospel javelin.** One was heard to say that if the Black Billy Sunday meetings were of the "Jim Crow order," God hasten the day when this class of Jim Crow-ism shall cover the land. **For here is an unusual sight never before witnessed in this section of good white Christian men and women not only singing and playing the instruments nightly, but when it comes to personal work, they throw aside every vestige of racial feelings and throw their arms around their black sister and brother and with weeping eyes and hearts full of love, lead them to Christ.** This is the kind of Jim Crow-ism one may witness any night in the Black Billy Sunday revival meetings, whether in Evanston or down in Texas. **Black Billy preaches the Gospel "that Christ is all and in all" as the only panacea for the world's ills.** Many on every side are heard to say that Black Billy's coming to Chicago and Evanston has been a godsend for whether in the trenches at San Juan Hill in 1898 or on the rostrum he has proven himself the same fearless foe, the terror to evildoers. He has preached old Gospel with a strange power, that has bade the natives sit up and take notice.

As this Sunday will mark the end of his stay in Evanston, it is predicted that if the Patton Gymnasium could be secured for a farewell demonstration, that a capacity audience would hear the final word of the eloquent soul winner before he beats trail back to his home in the Lone Star State, where thousands of both races await his coming with open arms.

In October 1896, J. Gordon McPherson proudly marched through the streets of Salt Lake City, UT, on his way to Fort Douglas as one of the members of the famous 24th Regiment; and from that time to the present, he and the writer have been warm friends. He faithfully served with that regiment in Cuba during the Spanish-American War in 1898, and greatly assisted to administer to the sick and the afflicted, he was right up in front and was in the thickest of the fighting when the members of that regiment made its long to be remembered charge up San Juan Hill amid shot and shell, which was falling all around them as thick and as fast as hail.

Not long after the close of the Danish-American War, he honorably severed bis connection with the 24th Regiment; and for several years thereafter, he resided in Salt Lake City, UT, where he was highly respected by all classes of its citizens.

An evangelist with an enviable war record, "The Fighting Parson," **Rev. Dr. J. Gordon McPherson, California's noted old-fashioned black revivalist, the Billy Sunday of the *black* race** is coming to Denver to lead a big, old-fashioned revival and stir the capitol city and awaken a deep moral and spiritual interest. Dr. McPherson is hero of the yellow fever camps of Cuba, and he comes with an unequaled record as one of the greatest old-time revivalists of his day, **the only living rival of "Billy Sunday," the famous baseball evangelist. Thousands of white and *black* people flock to hear this gifted *black* revivalist. At Colorado Springs, where he is leading a union evangelistic campaign, hundreds of white people battle nightly to gain admittance into Payne's Chapel, A. M. E. church, to hear this eloquent *black* preacher of the old-time Gospel. They come in automobiles and vehicles of various kinds. Nightly, hundreds crowd the sidewalks around the building to hear this mighty man of God.** Dr. David E. Overs and the people at Zion Baptist Church are to be commended for their foresight in securing this famous revivalist to lead a big, soul-winning campaign here in Denver at this time. Evangelist McPherson will close his Colorado Springs meeting in time to reach Denver to launch his campaign on Sunday, May 27, at Historic Zion Baptist Church, which is one of the large religious edifices in the Rocky mountain regions.

It is predicted that the capitol city will receive a mighty stirring at the hands of the "Black Billy Sunday," who has the record of attracting the largest crowds of any *black* revivalist in the world. His coming has stirred the religious forces of Denver, and it is predicted that a record-breaking crowd will greet the famous soul winner on his

arrival in the capitol city to lead the forces of righteousness against the Host of Sin.
The Denver Star., May 19, 1917, Image 4

BLACK BILLY SUNDAY

Great *Black* Spiritual Healer Whose Marvelous Cures by Divine Powers Has Startled Country

And **there is great joy throughout the city among the *black* folks by the announcement of the coming of the Famous *Black* Preacher, Healer, and Psychologist, who is known throughout the country as "Black Billy Sunday," but his real name being J. Gordon McPherson, and by many is considered the wonder of the age because of his marvelous powers of spiritual healing of pain and disease, by some he is called the Miracle Man or the Creole Wonder. This *black* preacher has traveled throughout the country, in Canada, the Isles of the Sea and has laid his gifted hands on thousands of afflicted and suffering whites and *blacks* who have been cured as if by a miracle.** Many poor human outcasts have been redeemed to society. **Dope fiends, drug and tobacco habits have been cured; those who are demon possessed with the evils of voodooism, the spells have been taken off, and the demon spirits cast out of their lives.** Many who have been unfortunate in the game of life have been blessed with happiness and success and are now happy and prosperous in business. As Billy will only be here for ten days, and will preach each evening at the Mt. Calvary Baptist Church, on Weeks Street, at 7:30, the public is most cordially invited. The first services will be held on this Sunday, October 1st, commencing with an old-fashioned sunrise prayer meeting for those seeking a deeper work of Grace, at the morning hour Billy will anoint and bless the sick and suffering ones who may come. He will preach at 11 AM, on the "Divine Touch," at 3 PM, a monster citywide mass meeting of the local pastors and their congregations. **At the evening hour, the subject will be on the "Pre-Eminence of Jesus Christ in the Solution of the World's Problems." As thousands flock to hear this wonderful *black* preacher, it is of importance that you come early to get a seat, as hundreds are turned away at every service**. Adv.

The Weekly Iberian., September 30, 1922, Image 5

CHAPTER 5

BLACK WOMEN IN MINISTRY

Throughout the ages, God has used many women of all races to make a difference for His Kingdom. We don't often hear many of their stories, so I decided to include two of them here.

If you are a woman, I pray that these accounts will inspire you to be all that God has called you to be today. God can and will use anyone whom He chooses to, for His greater purposes, if they are willing to be used. PAMELA

REMARKABLE *BLACK* WOMAN

Traveling Evangelist
Has Conducted More Meetings than Moody

Walker Lake bulletin., July 13, 1898, Image 4

Amanda Smith is a traveling evangelist who has conducted more revival meetings than Moody and covered more territory in a given space of time than most itinerant preachers. Moreover, she is a full-blooded African *Black*, although born and raised in this country. She is one of the most progressive and successful women of her race. She has by her own exertion recently bought and paid for an orphans' home in Chicago, at a cost to her of $10,000. After traveling through Africa and England from which she has but recently returned, her evangelistic work was resumed in this country. In 1890, Mrs. Smith wrote and published an autobiography, "The Story of the Lord's Dealings with Amanda Smith," together with an Introduction by Bishop Thoburn of India.
Lincoln County Leader., July 01, 1898, Image 6

Mrs. Amanda Smith, the greatest evangelist of the race, will preach at St. Peter's Church, June 10th, morning afternoon, and evening. Everyone is invited to attend all of the services.
The Appeal., June 09, 1900, Image 3

The editor of The INTELLIGENCER attended Zion Church last Friday night, and again on Sunday night, to hear the wonderful *black* woman evangelist, **Mrs. Lena Mason.** She is truly a wonder. While having but little education, she is well acquainted with the Bible and quotes it often to prove her points. She never hesitates for the right word, but talks rapidly; and often, she will speak for ten minutes at a time with an eloquence and force that would be wonderful coming from a highly educated person. The more eloquent she becomes the better language she uses, but when she drops to a conversational tune, her grammar takes wings. She has composed several very good songs, and she is a fine singer. She has a voice that can be heard all over any auditorium and says **she has preached to**

audiences of ten thousand people. Her voice never grows weak or husky. We're glad we heard her and are sorry that everybody in Lexington could not attend her wonderful meetings. She swayed her audience at will, and when her climaxes came, there were a hundred voices crying "amen." She was sharp, witty, and titled her sermon nicely to the needs of her congregation.
The Weekly Intelligencer., May 28, 1898, Image 3

Mrs. Lena Mason preached at Zion M. E. Church Thursday night, last night, and will continue till after next Thursday night. The sermon Thursday night was said to be wonderful. **She is a *black* woman, with but little education; and the question is, how does she come with such a flow of elegant, eloquent language?** White people are invited to attend these meetings, and arrangements have been made to accommodate all who may attend.
The Weekly Intelligencer., May 21, 1898, Image 3

REV. MRS. LENA MASON.

The American citizen. [volume] (Topeka, Kan.) 1888-1909, August 16, 1895, Image 1

NOTABLE WOMAN EVANGELIST

Mrs. Lena Mason will arrive in the city Tuesday the 25th and begin revival meetings at the A. M. E. church on the same evening. The meetings were to have begun on the 12th but were postponed on account of the sickness of Mrs. Mason. **It is said that Mrs. Mason is the greatest woman preacher the *black* race has ever produced. Many thousands have been won to Christ through her efforts.** The pastors and members of all churches with the public in general, are invited to attend take some active part in these meetings. The church is on the corner of Second and Jefferson Streets.
Arizona Republican., July 21, 1911, Page SIX, Image 6

BLACK WOMAN AN EVANGELIST

Preaches Like Sam Jones and Will Be Heard in St. Louis

A *black* woman evangelist, **Mrs. Lena Mason, who preaches the Gospel after the fashion of Sam Jones** and has waged war against sin in many of the principal cities of the United States, will commence revival meeting tomorrow at Old Union Church, Eleventh and Locust Streets. **She is termed "The World Wonder" among the *Blacks*,** and her humor is said to have given her distinction that no other woman evangelist ever enjoyed.

The Reverend B. W. Stewart, pastor of Wyman's Central Mission, and many other *black* ministers of St. Louis will enlist in her campaign here. **She is said to have converted 750 persons at Minneapolis during her revival there.** She also met with great success at Denver and Atlanta, GA.

The St. Louis Republic., June 15, 1902, PART II, Page 3, Image 17

Chapter 6

Young Gentlemen

In the following articles, you will read about Jimmy Washington. He was a young boy with an amazing ability to be able to memorize the Bible. He used his gift from God to advance the Kingdom of God. What I liked about the articles is that they show that God can use anyone no matter how young they are.

DEAN

"Let no one despise your youth, but be an example to the believers in word, in conduct, in love, in spirit, in faith, in purity."
1 Timothy 4:12

REMARKABLE MEMORY

Black Boy Can Recite 536 Chapters of the Bible

"Jimmy" Washington, 17 years old, the Black "Boy Preacher" and "Biblical Prodigy" who is in Kansas City to conduct revival services and deliver lectures at the different Black churches, **can repeat 536 chapters of the Bible**, he says, and remember the words of a song after hearing them twice. **Although he never went to school a day in his life, he can read, write, and speak good English. He has become known as the "Black Moody" and the "Walking Bible."** He has lectured before audiences in Carnegie Hall in New York and Tremont Temple in Boston.

Born in Little Rock, AR, in 1888, he asserts that at the age of five years he was favored with the gift of reading and speaking to his people by God. In telling of his powers, he said:

"I have no way of accounting for my natural ability except that it was a gift sent by God. My mother died when I was a month old. Not long after that, my father met with an accident that cost him his eyesight. My father secured the agency in Little Rock, AR, where we lived, for Rev. DeWitt Talmage's book, *From Manger to Throne*. By canvassing for the book, he made a living for us both.

"One day, when I was five years old, my father came home and threw one of the books on the floor. I was looking at the pictures when suddenly I began to read it with accuracy. My father heard me and was astounded. He took me in to several white men who had befriended him when he had lost his eyesight, and through their influence, I was called before the State Legislature of Arkansas. The legislatures took a deep interest in my powers as a mere child, and the result was that I was given a recommendation by the Legislature to preach, lecture, and read to my people.

"I began preaching as a child and have continued to the present time. The number of conversions in meetings at which I have spoken will exceed 5,000.

"I learned l to write from autographs of the white men to whom I was introduced. I would take the names and trace them. It was not long until I could write well.

"In mathematics I have no ability whatever. I can count from one to one hundred, but that is due to memory alone. I can neither add nor subtract, and multiplication is out of the question.

"While I can read, memorize, and recite everything in English, I find that the Bible is much easier for me to learn than anything else. I am gradually increasing the number of chapters of the Bible that I can repeat, and someday I hope to recite the whole Bible as well as any chapter that may be chosen at random." The Black "boy preacher" has achieved success as an evangelist at camp meetings. He asserts that his evangelistic power was given him by God. While he delivers lectures and sermons that he has prepared, he says he prefers speaking extemporaneously. His blind father accompanies him and helps in the evangelistic work by singing old plantation religious songs.—*Kansas City Star*
The Mt. Sterling Advocate., October 25, 1905, Image 4

I believe that likely this "Jimmie L. Washington" is the same young man, "Jimmy Washington," mentioned in the above article; because "Jimmie" was nine in this article in 1897, and "Jimmy" was 17 in the article above in 1905, so his age corresponds perfectly with the years listed.
DEAN

On next Monday night, our citizens will have an opportunity of hearing **Jimmie L. Washington**, the nine-year-old Black boy preacher. **The press generally pronounce him to be a wonder, and he draws large crowds wherever he goes.**
The Free Press., May 27, 1897, Image 3

MORE YOUNG, POWERFUL PREACHERS...

Tommy Brannon, an eight-year-old *Black* boy preacher of Chattanooga, has created a great sensation among the *Blacks* of Atlanta, GA. **Thousands flocked to hear him at every service.**
The Free Press. (Poplarville, MS), May 06, 1897, Image 2

Boy Preacher

Tommy Brannon the 8-year-old boy preacher of Chattanooga, Tenn., is doing good work known in Georgia, where he is holding Evangelistic meetings every night. The churches in which he preaches are not large enough to hold the crowds of people who go to hear him, and hundreds are turned away every night. A number of conversions are professed from the sermons he preaches.
The Appeal. [volume] (Saint Paul, Minn. ;) 1889-19??, May 08, 1897, Image 1

William Miller, a fourteen-year-old *Black* boy preacher, of Memphis, delivered a sermon on the square Saturday, preaching from the text, "Marvel not, ye must be 'borned' again."
The Columbia Herald., May 28, 1897, Page 5, Image 5

A *Black* boy preacher, only ten years old, has been holding a revival at Four Mile Church between here and Union City for the past week. **Large crowds attend each service, and those who have heard this precious Gospel expounder pronounce him a real wonder.**

The Richmond Climax., September 25, 1901, Image 3

The Lexington Herald of Thursday last says: "**Harry Inward Killerbrew**, the 11-year-old *Black* boy preacher of Covington, is holding a revival at Quinn Chapel and will continue through Sunday. He has been preaching since he was five years old."

The Hazel Green Herald., October 16, 1902, Image 1

Chapter 7

Healing Evangelists

Healing is an important avenue in the advancement of the Kingdom of God. The following articles cover two people who were known for their ability to be used of God in the laying on of hands and have the results of people being healed no matter what nationality they were.

DEAN

"And these signs will follow those who believe: In My name they will cast out demons; they will speak with new tongues; they will take up serpents; and if they drink anything deadly, it will by no means hurt them; they will lay hands on the sick, and they will recover."
Mark 16:17-18

Interesting News Items

A *black* divine healer is creating a sensation in the *black* quarters of New Decatur, AL. **Blacks come from many miles, and many remarkable cures are reported.**
Daily Public Ledger., February 02, 1900, Image 3

CROWD*ED* HOUSE BOAT, AGED *BLACK* HEALER

Native of Canada Has Power to Cure by Laying on of Hands

New Orleans, LA, April 1. Led by a score of crippled and ailing men and women, hundreds of persons crowded the Mississippi levee last night trying to reach the ramshackle houseboat of **John Cudney**, a kindling peddler, known as "Brother Isaiah," because of his reputed cures by the laying on of hands. Cudney is 73 years of age and a native of Canada. The press was so great that 35 policemen were assigned to keep order. On a rumor that Cudney was about to appear, there was a rush that bore five of the guards into the river. All were rescued. **Reports Thursday that the "healer" had restored sight to the blind started a rush to the levee. Many invalids were carried on cots, Cudney worked all night, retiring at dawn when in danger of physical collapse.** The rich came with the poor, but offers of money were refused. The authorities are taking no action against "Brother Isaiah," because he is neither prescribing medicines nor accepting fees.

The Dallas Express., April 03, 1920, Image 1

MULTITUDES FLOCK TO AGED HEALER "BROTHER ISAIAH" TO BE CURED OF ILLS

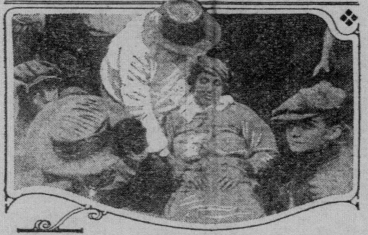

Photos show John Cudney, "Brother Isaiah," preaching to multitude near New Orleans and curing a woman paralyzed for years.

Thousands of persons have journeyed to the houseboat of John Cudney, called "Brother Isaiah" at his request, near New Orleans to seek his aid in being cured of ailments and afflictions. Many of his cures are said to be miraculous. He has cured blindness and helped many cripples to walk, say spectators. He says his cures are made through prayer and faith.

EASED THEIR PAINS

Black Preacher Does Public Healing in Shelby

Reverend Edwards, a *black* preacher and divine healer of Rocky Mount, preached in the courthouse Sunday afternoon to a crowd that filled the large auditorium, says the *Cleveland Star*. **Whites and blacks heard his impassioned sermon, and some of the white people declared that he is a great power with his race, his style of preaching being modelled after Billy Sunday, the world's most successful evangelist.** After the sermon, Edwards took a collection, then set about to heal those in his audience who went up to be healed, and after Edwards had waived his hand over their bodies and told them of his wonderful powers as a divine healer, they declared before the audience that all pain had left them and they felt sound and well again. One man who had been suffering with rheumatism was made to put aside his stick and a soldier in the recent World War who had been suffering with his side was relieved of his pain for a short time, but later the pain returned and the soldier went back to Edwards for another healing.

Edwards has created quite a stir among his race and received considerable newspaper notoriety on account of his hypnotic influence and his spectacular preaching.
Yorkville Enquirer., August 26, 1921, Image 1

CHAPTER 8

ENTIRE CITY SHUTS DOWN TO HONOR MAN OF GOD

The following is an account of a black pastor who made such an impact on the people of his city that the Mayor had all businesses shut down for thirty minutes to honor his life when he passed.
PAMELA

City to Stop Work for 30 Minutes
In Tribute to Dead *Black* Preacher

By the *Associated Press*.
COLUMBIA, SC. August 21. Columbia today, officially and privately, mourned the passing of **"Uncle Jaggers," 93-year-old *black* preacher**, who, for three-quarters of a century, has held the love and respect of the high and low, white and black.

Mayor W. A. Coleman, by proclamation, set aside 30 minutes from 3:30 until 4 o'clock, the time of the funeral, for suspension of business activities throughout the city; and representatives of all walks of life, from bootblack to most prominent citizen, arranged their affairs to enable them to pay tribute to the *black*'s memory. A fund has been started for erection of a memorial in his honor.

Born a slave, the Rev. Charles Jaggers of the African Methodist Episcopal Church began preaching "from the fence corners," as he put it, when he was 14; and **for 76 years he has never wavered from his one text, "Let this mind be in you, which was also in Jesus Christ," from Philippians 2:5.**

With contributions from white friends, he established a mission for his people and an "old folks' home," both of which he left free of debt; and *he* devoted much of his time to carrying the Gospel, once more, "from the fence corners," to the prisoners working in chain gangs.

At the end of each year, he accepted a salary of 1 cent. His services, he insisted, belonged to God. Not until the death of his wife, several weeks ago, did his health fail; and the best of hospital care was unable to restore his rugged voice to his calling.

Evening Star., August 21, 1924, Page 18, Image 18

Interesting history about Rev. Charles Jaggers' life:

"UNCLE" CHARLES JAGGERS

Ninety-Year-Old *Black* Missionary Now a Seminary Student

"Uncle" Charles Jaggers, famous *black* missionary of Columbia, made famous by a write-up given him in the *American Magazine* by the late Samuel C. Derieux, has assumed a new role. He is now a student of the Columbia Theological Seminary, institution of the Southern Presbyterian Church. He is "sitting in" on classes taught by several of the prominent theologians. "'Uncle' Jaggers is a great admirer of my white brethern" as he terms the divines of the seminary. He is ninety years old and says he is happier than he ever was in his life. He was a slave prior to the civil war.

The County Record., November 02, 1922, Image 8

CHAPTER 9

EARLY GIANTS OF FAITH IN AMERICA

What I like about this chapter is that you can read about many African-American apostles, prophets, evangelists, pastors, and teachers who were committed to getting the Gospel out to all people, even though they were slaves in the United States. This goes to show that God will get His Word out to people, no matter what the situation is. Not that we condone slavery, but God did not let slavery stop Him from making sure that every slave had the opportunity to have that freedom for eternity.

DEAN

"And He Himself gave some to be apostles, some prophets, some evangelists, and some pastors and teachers, for the equipping of the saints for the work of ministry, for the edifying of the body of Christ, till we all come to the unity of the faith and of the knowledge of the Son of God, to a perfect man, to the measure of the stature of the fullness of Christ;"
Ephesians 4:11-13

OUR GIANTS SPEAK
The Church in Afro-American Life

These are excerpts from *The Negro's Church* by Benjamin E. Mays and Joseph W. Nicholson. The publication of this book was sponsored by the Institute of Social and Religious Research, an independent agency organized in 1921 to apply scientific method to the study of social and religious subjects.

Achieving Freedom in the Church

The first negro church in America is reported to have been founded by one Mr. Palmer at Silver Bluff, South Carolina, between the years of 1773-1775. A kind master, George Galphin, is said to have become a patron of this congregation, and further to have permitted David George, a slave, to be ordained for this special work, after having formerly allowed George Liele to preach to this group.

The ministerial work of George Liele became of such importance that his master liberated him so that he might preach without interference. It is generally believed that he was instrumental in organizing the first *Black* Baptist church in the city of Savannah in about 1779.

Andrew Bryan, though frequently persecuted, was encouraged by his master to the extent that he was allowed to erect a wooden church on the land of Mr. Edmond Davis at Yamacraw. He so impressed the people with his Gospel messages that *blacks* and whites helped him to raise sufficient funds to purchase a lot upon which he erected a church. On this spot, the first African Baptist church of Savannah is known to have stood for years. Bryan purchased his freedom and continued his church work in and about Savannah.

In Virginia, between 1770 and 1800, many *blacks* won fame as forceful preachers. Among them were Gowan

Pamphlet, pastor of the Baptist church in Williamsburg; William Lemon, who was chosen by a white congregation to serve at the Pettsworth or Gloucester church; Josiah Bishop, who preached to a mixed audience in Portsmouth as early as 1795 and who so impressed his congregation that they gave him money with which to purchase his freedom; "Uncle Jack," who preached from plantation to plantation in Virginia, doing it so effectively that white citizens raised a fund with which they purchased his freedom; and in addition they bought him a farm where for more than forty years he continued his ministry and converted many white people; Henry Evans, a free *black* of Virginia, who preached so convincingly in Fayetteville, NC, that the town council gave up its opposition and allowed him to erect a Methodist church there in 1790; and finally John Stewart, a free *black* of Virginia, who went to Ohio and preached with so much power that he organized white people into a church in Marietta, Ohio.

In 1790, Lemuel Haynes preached to whites in Connecticut, Vermont, and Massachusetts [*and for the last 11 years of his life (1822-1833) at South Granville Congregational Church, Granville, New York*]. John Gloucester, a pioneer Presbyterian preacher, attracted the attention of Doctor Blackburn of Tennessee, who was converted by the preaching of this slave. Doctor Blackburn purchased Gloucester, encouraged him to study for the ministry and later granted him his freedom.

These illustrations, drawn from Dr. Woodson's History of the *Black* Church, are given to show that freedom in the *black*'s religious and church life had an early historical beginning, and that this fact has served to give "freedom in *black* church life" precedence over that freedom which the *black* is allowed to experience in other places of his life. Thus quite early the *Black* preached, highly restricted in other fields, achieved freedom in the church through his own initiative and sympathetic encouragement from white people and his own flock.

This achievement was another milestone in the *black*'s struggle for recognition and survival on the new continent. The freedom in his church, which the *black* merited and gained relatively early, while freedom in other realms was still denied him, has been one of the basic reasons for the rapid numerical growth of the *Black* in the United States.
[1]**The Buffalo Criterion, 2 January 1986**

We want to include the following two accounts of evangelists here as well.
DEAN & PAMELA

Black Evangelist Conducts a Successful Meeting Here

Rev. W Boliver David, the Georgia evangelist, has been conducting a very successful revival at the Baptist Church. The attendance has been good throughout the series of sermons, many white people being present and making talks. Quite a number of converts have already been secured.
The Hummer., September 28, 1917, Image 5

WILL PREACH TONIGHT
Market Square to Be Enlivened by a Black Evangelist

Rev. Henry Groves, a *Black* Evangelist of the Missionary Baptist Church, will hold services tonight on Market Square, beginning at 7 o'clock.

This revered gentleman has quite an interesting piece of history connected with his brief term in the ministry.

He was born and raised in Henderson, and is a coal miner by profession.

While at work in the mines at Empire, KY., the spirit called him to go forth and preach.

That was on the 28th day of last March.

He started on his preaching tour on the 25th of April, since which time he has walked over 1,300 miles, and has not missed a single day of preaching.

He came here last night from Portsmouth where he has been the past five weeks.

Daily public ledger. [volume], October 26, 1905, Image 1

CHAPTER 10
BLIND BUTLER
SINGING EVANGELIST

G. A. Butler, who was referred to as both [1]Professor and [2]Reverend in old newspaper articles, was a renowned evangelist singer in the early 1900s who sang in churches, revival meetings, and camp meetings in Kansas, Washington, Oregon, and Texas. He was a truly gifted and talented vocalist who amazingly impacted over 200,000 souls.
PAMELA

BLIND BUTLER,
The greatest Black Evangelist Singer in the world, will sing in the BIG TENT Camp Meeting, 19th Street, between Paseo and Lydia, Kansas City, Mo., beginning Sunday, June 3rd at 3 p. m. Every night in June. **Blind Butler has brought more than 200,000 souls to Christ through his singing** which is old fashioned, charming with his gestures and shouts, captivating because of the poetry and music in his singing. Thus you see we will have the old-time Camp Meeting where Grandma and Grandpa will have a chance to do some old-time shouting and the young people will be there to see it well done and also take a hand. Everybody invited. -Rev. A Morre, Secretary
The Kansas City Sun., June 02, 1917, Image 1

BLIND BUTLER,

The Kansas City Sun., June 02, 1917, Image 1

Chapter 11
George Washington Carver

As a young African American boy, I'd always heard of George Washington Carver and the genius that he was. He made a difference in my life back then. When I became a Christian and found out his love for God and how he credited God for all of his knowledge and inventions, he even made more of a huge difference in my walk and belief of God.
DEAN

As you will see in the last article in this chapter, George Washington Carver gave all the credit to God for every invention that he designed. These are his own words, "I didn't do it. God has only used me to reveal some of His wonderful providences." He walked in amazing humility, and no matter how God chooses to use us, we, likewise, should always give all the credit to Him.
PAMELA

"And Moses said to the children of Israel, 'See, the Lord has called by name Bezalel the son of Uri, the son of Hur, of the tribe of Judah; and He has filled him with the Spirit of God, in wisdom and understanding, in knowledge and all manner of workmanship, to design artistic works, to work in gold and

silver and bronze, in cutting jewels for setting, in carving wood, and to work in all manner of artistic workmanship.'"
Exodus 35:30-33

How a Missouri *Black* Won Success

Lawrence, MO. Recently, a young man inquired at *The Chieftain* office door for Mr. Woods' office. He was told he could see the name on the door on the opposite side of the hall. "But I can't read," he said. The editor was so nonplussed by his admission that he neglected to ask him if it were possible that he was reared in Lawrence County, with its hundred schools, and yet was unable to read so simple a word as "Woods!"

To those who think they have a good pretext for not having at least a rudimentary education, the following story of George Washington Carver will put their little excuses to shame. Born near the close of the Civil War in a little log cabin on the farm of Moses Carver at Diamond Grove, Newton County, of a *Black* mammy, who been the property of Mr. Carver and *Black* father belonging on a neighboring farm, he is today a professor at Tuskegee Institute and known throughout the South as the wizard chemist. His life story reads more like fiction than fact.

In the closing days of the war, George and his mother were carried away by raiders. The kind-hearted Mr. Carver sent a man on horseback with money to obtain their release. When he reached the marauders, Mary Carver had gone on; and he was unable to locate her, nor was her son ever able to find her afterward. He found George seriously ill with whooping cough. He was brought back to Mr. Carver who reared him. When a little tot, he became the happy possessor of an old blue-back speller, which he soon knew almost by heart. The only *black* school in the county was at Neosho, eight miles away, which he was able to attend when ten years old. Then began his struggle for an education. He begged passage on a wagon going to Fort Scott, Kans., and his real schooling began there. He worked in private families and did laundry work. After nine years of it, he went to Minneapolis, KS, where he finished his high school course. He then ran a laundry three years to obtain money to attend college. In the Iowa State College, he secured the degrees of bachelor and master of arts. After graduation he was given charge of a greenhouse, bacteriological laboratory and work in systematic botany. Thirty years ago, his work came to the attention of Booker T. Washington, who called him to Tuskegee where he has since labored.

This wizard chemist has evolved 150 products from the humble peanut alone. Some of them are 17 kinds of wood stains, dyes for cloth, oils of many kinds, lard, meal, flour, instant coffee, breakfast foods, axle grease, oil soap, linoleum, cheese filler, printer's ink, stock food, etc.

Some months ago, when the ways and means committee at Washington was considering the placing of a tariff on peanuts, quite a number of the 10 minute speakers appeared before it, last of all a smiling, soft-voiced black man, who woke up the tired, bored listless committee. He spoke ten minutes, and then bowed and smiled and gathered up his materials. "Give us more," they cried. When he stopped, he had talked an hour and forty minutes, and still they wanted more.

This man was Professor George Washington Carver of Tuskegee Institute, Alabama, the erstwhile little Newton County, Missouri, Black, a dreamer, an inventor, a scientist, who forced his way to an education when opportunities and schools for his race were as scarce as the proverbial hen's teeth.

How small in comparison are the efforts required of a white boy today!

A *BLACK* GENIUS

Richmond Times-Dispatch.

Not only his race, but the entire South takes pride in the achievements of that *black* wizard of chemistry, Prof. George Washington Carver, of Tuskegee. In recognition of his monumental work, the National Association for the Advancement of Colored People has awarded Carver the Spingarn Medal, a testimonial of worth most highly prized by his race. It is a deserved tribute to his genius.

Carver worked quietly at his institution made famous by Booker T. Washington, claims his discoveries will change the economic conditions of life in the South. He is said to have made 118 products from the sweet potato and 165 from the peanut. In his chosen field of agricultural chemistry, the Alabama *Black* ranks high among the laboratory wizards of the world.

In the career of Carver, there is inspiration and a lesson for every Southern *Black*. The advantages we had were no greater than those that come to thousands of others of his race. He was determined to make the most of the opportunities he had. He has succeeded surprisingly well. And he has remained in the South, where the *black* is better understood and regarded more sympathetically than in any section of the country.

Watauga Democrat., October 18, 1923, PAGE THREE, Image 3

ONE TIME SLAVE, NOW SCIENTIFIC WIZARD

An Astounding Story of George Carver's Life and Work

"AS A LITTLE CHILD"
(*one section of a much larger article*)

These facts would seem to indicate that George Carver's personality is as unique as his history. It is. **He combines in the most surprising way the simplicity of a child, the humility of a devout faith, and the confidence of scientific certainty.** His first words are likely to impress you as almost childish. Then you become conscious of an unfathomable vein of mysticism and faith. Finally, you yield to speechless wonder as he opens for you a few windows into the scientific maze where his feet are so much at home. A true *black*, spare and thin, with a piping voice and a manner almost painfully modest, his clothing plain and none too new, a sprig of cedar in his button hole, **he is a striking figure indeed, but not distinguished by any of the expected marks of genius.**

Asked how he has made so many astounding discoveries, he promptly tells you, "I didn't do it. God has only used me to reveal some of His wonderful providences." All His work has been done in that spirit. Chemistry is its physical basis, but faith is its inspiration, prayer its atmosphere, and service its motive. To George Carver there is no conflict between science and religion.
Richmond Planet., March 29, 1924, Page 2, Image 2

Chapter 12

Destined for Greatness

During the course of my research, I became aware that there was a newspaper entitled the "Northwestern Bulletin-appeal," which ran weekly articles about men and women of color who made a difference in the history of America. I began reading through the stories and found them to be very interesting, so I decided to share some of their accounts with you here in this book.

You may or may not have read about these people in our current history books, nonetheless, these men and women left a behind a wonderful legacy that is still impacting our world today; for we are all interconnected, whether we realize it or not.
PAMELA

AMERICANIZATION SERIES

The *Bulletin-Appeal* will publish, each week, biographies and auto-biographies of men and women of the race who have contributed something worthwhile to the history of our common country. The object of these articles is to acquaint the youth of the race, both native born and alien, with facts that are not to be found in the average school history.

There are in the United States a large number of aliens of the *Black* races. The immigration laws limit the number of whites of each nationality, forbids Orientals, but permits the darker races to enter without restrictions. This fact is due, no doubt, out of deference to the American *Black*. It devolves a duty, however, upon the race to prepare the newcomers for American citizenship. That they may know America better, we present the biography of Benjamin Banneker, astronomer, mathematician, and surveyor:

BENJAMIN BANNEKER

[1]*The first book that Benjamin Banneker ever purchased was the Bible, and there was no book that he valued more highly than the Scriptures.*
PAMELA

Benjamin Banneker was born on a plantation in the state of Maryland, November 9, 1731. He died at Washington, DC, in the year 1806. His mother was a slave, and he was the son of the master. His paternal grandmother took unusual interest in young Benjamin, owing to his precocity and taught him to read and write. He received just enough of the rudiments of knowledge gained through his ability to read, to awaken a latent thirst to acquire an education. With the death of his father, which occurred in his early youth, he and his mother were given their freedom; and Benjamin set about to earn support for his mother and himself. He found employment with a surveyor as a chain-man and proved himself capable. He was deficient, however, in mathematics and at the age of 50 took up the study of the higher branches, such as algebra, geometry, and trigonometry. In a remarkably short time, he mastered this difficult science and rose to the highest degree as a surveyor. **Through his mastery of mathematics, he studied astronomy and became equally efficient in this science, as he had become as a surveyor. His investigations and discoveries**

attracted wide attention. Savants from Europe came to this country to consult with him. So learned was he that, even at that early time, the question of his race was not a barrier. Scientists were few in the world at that time, and Banneker, a *Black*, was regarded as one of the foremost. As a young man he attracted the attention of Thomas Jefferson and became his protege. He was on terms of intimacy with George Washington, Benjamin Franklin, Samuel Adams, John Adams, John Quincy Adams, and other celebrities. He was delegated by the President as one of a distinguished committee to determine the boundaries of the city of Washington and assisted materially in laying out the streets that today beautify the nation's capital. In 1792, he began the publication of "Banneker's Almanac," which contained many interesting things on science, as well as domestic matter. It is safe to say that he was the father of our weather bureau. His almanac was looked upon as a national institution and was continued up to the time of his death. Archaeologists are agreed that the mother of civilization was in Africa. The wise men of Ethiopia, Carthagena, and Egypt were adept in philosophy, mathematics, and astronomy. It was but natural for one of this lineage to take to the mastery of these subjects in the person of Benjamin Banneker.

Someday the American conscience will awaken to a sense of justice — someday the scales will strike a balance, and Benjamin Banneker will be mentioned in the textbooks of our schools and universities. Owing to racial prejudice, this man, who was the contemporary of the most eminent scientists of his day, will be accorded the place in history he so richly deserves. Had he lived in France, he would have been awarded a place among the "immortals" in the Hall of Fame.

The Northwestern Bulletin-appeal., January 31, 1925, Image 2

FREDERICK DOUGLASS

[2]Frederick Douglass was a licensed preacher in the African Methodist Episcopalian Zion church. He said this: [3]"I love the religion of Christianity - which cometh from above - which is a pure, peaceable, gentle, easy to be entreated, full of good fruits, and without hypocrisy."
DEAN

Frederick Douglass was the son of a *Black* mother who was a slave.

He was born on a plantation at Tuckahoe, MD, February 1817; he died at Washington, DC, February 20, 1895. It is fitting that the race should celebrate both the birth anniversary and the memorial of this great leader each year at this time.

His father was a white man and his master. In 1832, he was sold to a Baltimore ship builder, but made his escape in 1838.

He had taught himself to read and write, and changed his name from Frederick Augustus Bailey to Douglass. He worked as a day laborer in New York City, and in New Bedford, MA, where he became a member of an Anti-slavery Society, and later, one of its lecturers. His natural ability as an orator attracted wide attention, and he joined the ranks of Garrison, Phillips, Lovejoy, and other prominent speakers interested in the abolishment of slavery. In 1845, he published his autobiography and afterwards made a successful lecturing tour of England, where he created sentiment favorable to the cause for which he labored.

His freedom was bought while he was abroad. In 1870, he edited a journal entitled, *The National New Era*; in 1871, he was appointed by President Grant, secretary of the committee to San Domingo. In 1872, he was a presidential elector. President Hayes appointed him in 1877 to the office of U. S. Marshal for the District of Columbia, then Commissioner of Deeds. In 1889, he was appointed U. S. Minister to Haiti by President Harrison.

His autobiography was revised and enlarged in 1882 under the title of Life and Times of Frederick Douglass.

The late Dr. Booker T. Washington wrote a very interesting biography of Frederick Douglass which was published in 1907.

Douglass was an intellectual giant, possessed of logic and unusual common sense. As an orator, he had but few equals and was known for flowery eloquence and biting sarcasm. It was Douglass who created the term now in use to designate a degree of loyalty to the republican party. At a great republican gathering where he was called upon to speak, he began in the following manner:

"Ladies and Gentlemen, I am a republican; I am a loyal republican," (applause); "I am a black republican" (prolonged applause). This latter sentence was spoken after the second loud acclaim ceased, with a sardonic smile, for which he was famous. Thus, we have today the anomaly of white men who pride themselves upon being "black republicans."
The Northwestern Bulletin-appeal., February 21, 1925, Image 2

PHILLIS WHEATLEY
Poetess

[4]Phillis Wheatley was a devout Christian. She became a believer at the age of 16 and attended the

Old South Congregational Church in Boston. Besides being a notable apologist and abolitionist, she also funded missionary work in both Ghana and Siera Leone.

PAMELA

Phillis Wheatley was born in Africa about 1753. She died at Boston, MA, Dec. 5, 1794. When a mere child, she was brought to Boston by slave traders and sold to Mrs. John Wheatley, a kindly Christian woman. Phillis was taught to read and write and exhibited a fondness for books. Mrs. Wheatley and her daughters, taking unusual interest in teaching the little slave girl, she acquired, for the time, a superior education, reading Latin with facility. At an early age, she began to express her thoughts in verse, and some of her poems written at fourteen years of age give evidence of poetic ability. At nineteen, in the bloom of her youth, she visited England, where she attracted much attention. A volume of her poems dedicated to the Countess of Huntington was published there, containing her portrait and bearing the title, *Poems on Various Subjects, Religious and Moral, by Phillis Wheatley, (black) servant to Mr. John Wheatley of Boston, in New England*. After her return from England, she published several other poems, among others an address to General Washington. Her book was reprinted in Boston and passed through several editions. The family of Mr. Wheatley was broken up by death soon after her return. She was married to a man of her race by the name of Peters. She passed away without issue. Her poems contain a pathetic sweetness, such as only a soul could give forth under the peculiar circumstances that surrounded her life. **Her sentient nature and strong religious convictions as expressed in her writings combine beautifully the material with the spiritual.**
The Northwestern Bulletin-appeal., February 07, 1925, Image 2

DANIEL ALEXANDER PAYNE
Theologian

Here's a man of great achievements in advancing the Kingdom of God. Many of those accomplishments produced great results so that others could also step up in the Kingdom of God to become all God created them to be.
DEAN

> *"And whatever you do, do it heartily, as to the Lord and not to men,"*
> *Colossians 3:23*

Daniel Alexander Payne was born of slave parents at Charlestown, SC, February 24, 1811. At an early age, his parents were given their freedom at their owner's death. The family moved to Philadelphia, where young Payne received his primary education. After preliminary study, he entered the Lutheran Theological Seminary at Gettysburg, PA, but owing to trouble with his eyes, was not able to complete the course required for graduation. **He entered the Lutheran ministry in 1838, and in 1843,** *he* **became an itinerant minister of the African Methodist Episcopal Church. He was elected historiographer of his denomination in 1848, and in 1852 a bishop.** In March 1863, he was instrumental in purchasing for the African Methodist Episcopal Church the property of Wilberforce University, near Xenia, Greene County, Ohio. The school was reopened July 3, 1863, by Professor John G. Mitchell; and Bishop Payne became President, holding this office until his resignation in June 1876, when he was succeeded by Rev. Benjamin F. Lee, and then became chancellor and dean of the theological seminary. The growth of the university progressed steadily, notwithstanding a setback in 1865 from the destruction of the building by fire.

During 1867-68, Bishop Payne made a tour of Europe; was president of the organization of the Methodist Pastors' Association in Paris, France, in 1868, and in 1881 a delegate to the Methodist Ecumenical Council in London. He was a lifelong student and wrote several works of enduring value, among them are "History of the African Methodist Episcopal Church" (1865); "Recollections of Men and Things" (1877), and "Domestic Education" (1886). Lincoln University gave him the degree of LL.D. in 1879.

He was married in 1847 to Julia A. Bancroft, and after her death, to Eliza J. Morris in 1854. He died at Wilberforce, OH, Nov. 29, 1893.

Bishop Payne was a man of scholarly attainments and an eloquent pulpit orator. Though of small and delicate physique, he possessed executive qualifications of a high degree. He was a strict disciplinarian and exerted an influence that had much to do with the molding of the honorable character of the student body. The atmosphere of Wilberforce has always been wholesome, for which condition Daniel A. Payne was a large contributor.
The Northwestern Bulletin-appeal., May 16, 1925, Image 2

BOOKER T. WASHINGTON

This is a powerful quote by this very Godly man: "I will permit no man to narrow and degrade my soul by making me hate him. An even far greater legacy is that of our dear Lord, Jesus Christ. He changed the world during his 33 years on earth. He revealed God to us through His life, teachings, death and resurrection."

PAMELA

Booker Taliaferro Washington was born in slavery near Hales' Ford, Franklin County, VT, February 1858; died Nov. 14, 1915. After the Civil War, he went to Malden, WV, where he worked, first in a salt furnace and afterward in a coal mine; obtained some rudiments of education in a night school there, and finally after many difficulties, recounted in the autobiography "Up from Slavery" (1901), got to Hampton Normal and Agricultural Institute, Hampton, VA, where he studied in 1875-76. After a two year interval of teaching at Malden, he obtained further training at the Wayland Seminary, Washington, DC, and in 1879 was made instructor at Hampton. He had charge of the work of the Indian pupils then being experimentally introduced into the institution and established the night school as a regular and successful feature of the institute. In 1881, he was selected by Gen. S. C. Armstrong of Hampton on the application of citizens of Tuskegee, AL, to start in that place an institution on the plan of Hampton. The state legislature granted an appropriation of $2,000 annually for the salaries of the teaching force, but the Tuskegee Normal and Industrial Institute then existed in name only, without land, buildings, or credit. Washington, with himself as the only instructor, opened the school with an enrollment of 80, in an old church and a shanty. Later, he purchased a plantation about a mile from Tuskegee and removed the school thither to its present site. In 1918, the institution had 191 officers and instructors, 1451 students and over 2500 graduates. Its development was due chiefly to the activity of Washington in bringing the nature and merits of the work to public attention, and the originality and effectiveness of his methods. He aimed to give his race a practical education along lines of trade and industry, leading to an ultimate position of economic independence in the South. If this were attained, he asserted, political rights now denied would not be long withheld. He became well known as a forceful public speaker, his most noteworthy address probably being that given in 1895 at the opening of the Cotton States and Industrial Exposition in Atlanta, GA. He organized the National *Black* Business League at Boston in 1900. Among his writings are "The Future of the American *Black*" (1899); "Up from Slavery" (1901), the interesting autobiographical narrative referred to above; "Character Building" (1902), collected addresses to pupils of Tuskegee; "The Man Farthest Down" (1912). Several biographies have been written on the life and work of this remarkable man since his death. Dr. Washington's greatness was due to his wonderful constructive ability, his tenacity of purpose, courage of his convictions, practical common sense, and lofty idealism.

The Northwestern Bulletin-appeal., February 28, 1925, Image 2

WILLIAM SAUNDERS SCARBOROUGH
Philologist

William Saunders Scarborough was a remarkable Christian man when it came to education. He achieved and did so much to advance his nationality and beliefs that he became a great example for many of us today.
DEAN

"Wisdom is the principal thing; Therefore get wisdom. And in all your getting, get understanding.
The heart of the prudent acquires knowledge,
And the ear of the wise seeks knowledge."
Proverbs 18:15 and 4:7

William Saunders Scarborough was born at Macon, GA, February 16, 1852, son of Jeremiah and Frances S. Scarborough. He was educated in the schools of the American Missionary Association, the Lewis High School, Atlanta University, and Oberlin College.

Upon his graduation at Oberlin in 1875, he became instructor of Latin, Greek, and Mathematics at the Lewis High School and then devoted several months in the study of Hebrew and Greek at the Oberlin Theological Seminary. During vacations, he taught in the *Black* Normal Schools of Southern Ohio. From the theological school, he went to Payne Institute, Cokesbury, SC, as principal. In 1877, he was called to Wilberforce where he became professor of the Greek language and literature.

Professor Scarborough applied himself assiduously to the mastery of languages, for which he had a natural aptitude. In addition to a thorough knowledge of Latin, Greek, and Hebrew, he became familiar with Sanskrit, Gothic, Zend, Lithuanian, and old Slavonic, and was equally at home in the literature of the French, German, Italian, and Spanish languages.

He was the third of his race to be elected to a membership in the American Philological Association and the first selected to read a paper before that body. He is a member of the American Social Science, dialect and folk lore societies; the American Spelling Reform Association, the Modern Language Association; the Archaeological Institute of America, American Academy of Political and Social Science; Royal Society of Arts, London, England, and vice-president of the American *Black* Academy. Professor Scarborough was vice-president and head of the classical department at Wilberforce University for some years. From 1908 to 1920, he was president of the institution. President Harding appointed him as assistant in farm studies, U. S. Department of Agriculture. He is president emeritus of Wilberforce and exegetical editor of the Sunday School and tract publications of the A. M. E. Church. He was delegate to the Ecumenical Methodist Conference at London in 1901, 1921; delegate to the Congress of Races at London in 1911. He was a representative of the American Philological Conference held at Cambridge University in 1921.

He was postmaster of Wilberforce, Ohio, in 1879; one of the first of his race to advocate and assist in the organization of the *Black* Rights Convention of Columbus, Ohio, in 1883, and also various leagues having for their object the civil rights of the *Black* people. He was a member of the Republican State Central Committee for Ohio in 1879; in 1884, he was a delegate to the Methodist Centennial Conference at Baltimore; was chosen to address the *Black* Inter-State Conference at Pittsburgh in 1884.

As a scholar, Professor Scarborough stands pre-eminent. The degrees of A.M. and LL.D. were conferred upon him by Oberlin College in 1875-1878; LL.D. in 1882 by Liberia College; Ph.D. by Kentucky State University, 1892; Ph.D., Morris Brown College, 1908; F.Ph., St. Columba's College (England), 1909.

He married August 2, 1881, Miss Sarah C. Bierce of Danby, NY, a graduate of the Oswego Normal School and Principal of the Normal and Industrial Department at Wilberforce.

Professor Scarborough is the author of the following published volumes: *First Lessons in Greek* (1881); *Theory and Function of the Thematic Vowel in the Greek Verb* (1884); *Birds of Aristophanes* (1886); *A Theory of Interpretation* (1886); *Questions on Latin Grammar* (1889); *Andocides Orations* (1892); and a number of pamphlets. He has been a contributor to leading magazines and educational publications on the race question, classical, philosophical, and archaeological subjects. His Greek books are used as textbooks by Harvard and other leading universities and colleges.

Professor Scarborough resides at Wilberforce, where he enjoys the respect of the entire alumni and student body of the schools he has labored so well to develop. He is an outstanding figure in the field of education. In his particular specialty, he is without doubt the foremost man of the race. He exemplifies the best in student life and is proof sufficient that the American *Black* is capable of higher education.

The Northwestern Bulletin-appeal., June 20, 1925, Image 2

[5]*William Saunders Scarborough was a member of the African Methodist Episcopal Church, where he was a trustee and the Sunday School Superintendent.*

PAMELA

Chapter 13

Harriet Tubman

Woman of Deep Faith
and
Modern-day Moses

Harriet Tubman 'till this day is an inspiration in my walk with Christ. My first encounter of hearing about her was in the fifth grade when we were given a project that required us to write about someone in history. My teacher, at the time, suggested that I do my assignment on Harriet. Since then, I have looked into her life over and over again. When I found out about her commitment to Jesus Christ years ago, it was one of the most joyful discoveries I have ever known. To read of her loyalty to the Lord, God Almighty, has increased my dedication to my loving Heavenly Father. I pray you get the same or even better inspiration from what you're about to read about Harriet and her faithfulness to God Almighty.
DEAN

"I commend to you Phoebe our sister, who is a servant of the church in Cenchrea, that you may receive her in the Lord in a manner worthy of the saints, and assist her in whatever business she has need of you; for indeed she has been a helper of many and of myself also."
Romans 16:1-2

Harriet's religious character, I have not yet touched upon. Brought up by parents possessed of strong faith in God, she had never known the time, I imagine, when she did not trust Him and cling to Him, with an all-abiding confidence. She seemed ever to feel the Divine Presence near, and she talked with God "as a man talketh with his friend." Hers was not the religion of a morning and evening prayer at stated times, but when she felt a need, she simply told God of it and trusted Him to set the matter right.

"And so," she said to me, "as I lay so sick on my bed, from Christmas till March, I was always praying for poor ole master. 'Pears like I didn't do nothing but pray for ole master. 'Oh, Lord, convert ole master; Oh, dear Lord, change dat man's heart and make him a Christian.' And all the time he was bringing men to look at me, and dey stood there saying what dey would give, and what dey would take, and all I could say was, 'Oh, Lord, convert ole master.' Den I heard dat as soon as I was able to move I was to be sent with my brudders, in the chain-gang to de far South. Then I changed my prayer, and I said, 'Lord, if you ain't never going to change dat man's heart, kill him, Lord, and take him out of de way, so he won't do no more mischief.' Next ting I heard ole master was dead; and he died just as he had lived, a wicked, bad man. Oh, den it 'peared like I would give de world full of silver and gold, if I had it, to bring dat pore soul back, I would give myself; I would give eberyting! But he was gone, I couldn't pray for him no more."

As she recovered from this long illness, a deeper religious spirit seemed to take possession of her than she had ever experienced before. She literally "prayed without ceasing." "'Pears like, I prayed all de time," she said, "about my work, eberywhere; I was always talking to de Lord. When I went to the horse-trough to wash my face, and took up de water in my hands, I said, 'Oh, Lord, wash me, make me clean.' When I took up de towel to wipe my face and hands, I cried, 'Oh, Lord, for Jesus' sake, wipe away all my sins!' When I took up de broom and began to sweep, I groaned, 'Oh, Lord, whatsoebber sin dere be in my heart, sweep it out, Lord, clar and clean;' but I can't pray no more for pore ole master." No words can describe the pathos of her tones as she broke into these words of earnest supplication.

HARRIET The Moses of Her People, **1886, Pages 23-25,**
By Sarah H. Bradford

HARRIET TUBMAN
Abolitionist and Philanthropist

Harriet Tubman was born in slavery about 1815; she died at Auburn, NY, March 10, 1913.

She escaped from her master's plantation in Maryland when 25 years of age, visited Garrison, Brown, and other abolitionists and became an active promoter of the "Underground Railway."

She first rescued her parents, and during the two decades before the Civil War, made repeated journeys to the South and brought a total of 400 or more of her race to the North and Canada.

During the war, she served with distinction as a scout with the Massachusetts troops and guided Colonel Montgomery in his memorable expedition into South Carolina.

By the friendly help of Secretary Seward, she was enabled to make her home at Auburn, NY, after the war; and there, soon became engaged in philanthropic service on behalf of the poor and aged of her race.

Her efforts led to the "Foundation of the Harriet Tubman Home for Indigent *Black*s," to which she gave personal oversight until 1908.

She married in the South, in early life, a man named Tubman, who died, and later married Nelson Davis.

Harriet Tubman's service to her race and country are without parallel in like achievement by any member of her sex in the history of the world.

Her busy, helpful life and innate modesty, precluded her from writing an autobiography, even though importuned from time to time by her friends to do so.

When hatred and prejudice has spent its force and the era of brotherly love has taken possession of the American mind, Harriet Tubman, will be accorded her rightful place in history, along with Florence Nightingale, Clara Barton, Frances Willard, Susan B. Anthony, and the galaxy of other notable women.

It is to be hoped that from the pen of some one of the race, a biography of Harriet Tubman will soon issue and be given to the world. Her deeds of self-sacrifice and daring are an inspiration to the youth of the race.

It is very gratifying to note that St. Paul boasts of a civic league, among our group, that bears the honored name of this splendid character.

The Northwestern Bulletin-appeal., February 14, 1925, Image 2

Memorial To Harriet Tubman

Auburn, N. Y., June 16. High tribute was paid to the memory of the late Harriet Tubman, familiarly known as "Aunt Harriet," on Friday evening, June 12, when a large bronze tablet, a token of love and esteem of the citizens of Auburn, was unveiled at the Auditorium Theatre. The tablet, which has been placed in the county courthouse, bears the following inscription:

> **In Memory of**
> **HARRIET TUBMAN**
> **Born a slave in Maryland about 1821.**
> **Died in Auburn, N. Y.**
> **March 10, 1913.**
> **This Tablet is Erected by the Citizens**
> **of Auburn, 1914.**

…**Called the "Moses" of her people during the Civil War, with rare courage, she led over three hundred *black*s up from slavery to freedom and rendered invaluable service as nurse and spy. With implicit trust in God, she braved every danger and overcame every obstacle, withal she possessed extraordinary foresight and judgment so that she truthfully said: "On my underground railroad I nebber run my train off de track, and I nebber los a passenger."**

…**"Born as she was in the obscurity of slavery and bound by its shackles, the memory of this woman should be *an* object of reverence to every member of her race, and the example in her achievement an inspiration to every member of our great nation."**…
The Colorado Statesman., June 27, 1914, Image 1

Harriet Tubman's life; which was characterized by her GREAT FAITH, compassion, courage, strength, and determination, is a wonderful example for men and women today. She made great sacrifices in order to save many people of her race, and her life of self-sacrifice makes me think of Jesus Christ who made the ultimate sacrifice to save people of all races.

PAMELA

Chapter 14

What Are You Called To Do?

The Word of the Lord to the prophet, Jeremiah: "**Before I formed you in the womb, I knew you; Before you were born, I sanctified you; I ordained you a prophet to the nations**." Jeremiah 1:5 (NKJV)

"For I know the thoughts that I think toward you, saith the LORD, thoughts of peace, and not of evil, **to give you an expected end**." Jeremiah 29:11 (KJV)

God had a plan for Jeremiah's life before He even formed him in the womb. He had a plan for the disciples' lives, for the courageous men and women whom you read about in this book, and He has a plan for your life as well.

Consider the determination and perseverance of many of these former slaves to fulfill God's plans and purposes for their lives. They had great zeal that carried them through the hardships that they had to endure—many things that most of us have never even come close to experiencing.

Be encouraged, my friend, God created you with special plans and purpose for your life as well. Just like He did with these black men and women who lived over 100 years ago, God wants to use you, too!

"WHAT IS MY PURPOSE OR MY CALL?"

It is partially your position in your family, but it goes far beyond that. Each one of us was born with a call on our lives, to make a difference for eternity. Many people just don't realize how important their calls are.

If you don't already know what yours is, you need to seek God about this. He wants to reveal your call to you, fill you with His Spirit, and empower you to walk in it. He created you for relationship with Him and to walk in your calling!

If our forefathers hadn't walked in their callings, God would have given their God-given purposes to others. He will find a way for His will to be accomplished on Earth; however, He may need to do it differently than His first plan, because we have free will. The choice is ours, whether or not to walk in our call. He won't force us.

Each of our lives is intertwined with many other people. We all have a circle of influence. If we look at every day as an opportunity to partner with God, then we will realize that He wants to use us to make a difference for His Kingdom.

Remember that God often used people who didn't measure up to the standards of the "religious" people of the time in which they were living in. He specializes in using those who feel unqualified or who don't think they measure up to the world's standards.

"For you see your calling, brethren, that **not many wise according to the flesh, not many mighty, not many noble, are called**. But God has chosen the foolish things of the world to put to shame the wise, and God has chosen the weak things of the world to put to shame the things which are mighty; and the base things of the world and the things which are despised God has chosen, and the things which are not, to bring to nothing the things that are, that no flesh should glory in His presence. But of Him you are in Christ Jesus, who became for us wisdom from God—and righteousness and sanctification and redemption—that, as it is written, 'He who glories, let him glory in the LORD.'" 1 Corinthians 1:26-31 (NKJV)

Lemuel Haynes was a man of humble beginnings. He surrendered his entire life to Jesus; and God used him powerfully to reach many people with the Good News of the Gospel of Jesus Christ.

"Can there be a more delightful employment, this side of heaven, than to send the blessed news of Salvation to a perishing world?"
Lemuel Haynes

**WALK IN YOUR CALLING
AND FULFILL YOUR CALL!**

In Closing

We pray that this book has challenged you about the seriousness of your commitment level to God. The examples of these men and women's lives really put things in perspective about what matters for eternity. Remember that God wants to use YOU for Kingdom purposes ... FOR A SUCH A TIME AS THIS.

May God bless you, prepare you, strengthen you, lead you, guide you, give you wisdom, and use you to help bring in the final harvest of souls in these last days in which we're living.

SALVATION PRAYER

If you don't already know Jesus as your Lord and Savior and you want to, please pray the following prayer from your heart to enter into a relationship with Him:

Dear Jesus,
I admit that I'm a sinner, and I need You. Thank you for dying on the cross in my place and taking my punishment. Please forgive me for my sins, and come into my heart and be my Savior and my Lord. Please help me to live for You from this day forward. Thank you for making me part of Your family. In Jesus' Name, Amen.

If you prayed this prayer sincerely from your heart, you are now a child of God. You have just taken your first step in your journey with Him. Welcome to His family

BIBLIOGRAPHY

Chapter 1: God's Heart for Revival and Awakening

1. The Detroit Tribune, February 10, 1040 - Accessed Date: November 22, 2024

Chapter 9: Early Giants of Faith in America

The Buffalo Criterion, 2 January 1986 Used with permission by e-mail on January 14, 2025.

Chapter 10: BLIND BUTLER Singing Evangelist

1. The Holt County sentinel., September 17, 1897, Image 1 Accessed Date: January 23, 2025

2. The Dallas express. [volume], May 13, 1922, PAGE SIX, Image 6 Accessed Date: January 23, 2025

Chapter 13: Destined for Greatness

1. https://www.acton.org/pub/religion-liberty/volume-20-number-2/benjamin-banneker - Accessed Date: November 22, 2024

2. https://oll.libertyfund.org/publications/liberty-matters/2021-02-11-frederick-douglass-and-the-black-christian-experience - Accessed Date: January 25, 2025

3. https://www.azquotes.com/author/4104-Frederick_Douglass/tag/christianity - Accessed Date: January 25, 2025

4. https://www.thegospelcoalition.org/article/meet-phillis-wheatley/ - Accessed Date: November 22, 2024

5. https://en.wikipedia.org/wiki/William_Sanders_Scarborough - Accessed Date: November 22, 2024

Made in the USA
Columbia, SC
28 March 2025

55772888R00063